James Joyce and Classical Modernism

Classical Receptions in Twentieth-Century Writing

Series Editor: Laura Jansen
Each book in this groundbreaking new series considers the influence of antiquity on a single writer from the twentieth century. From Woolf to Walcott and Fellini to Foucault, the modalities and texture of this modern encounter with antiquity are explored in the works of authors recognized for their global impact on modern fiction, poetry, art, philosophy, and socio-politics.

A distinctive feature of twentieth-century writing is the tendency to break with tradition and embrace the new sensibilities of the time. Yet the period continues to maintain a fluid dialogue with the Greco-Roman past, drawing on its rich cultural legacy and thought, even within the most radical movements that ostentatiously questioned and rejected that past. Classical Receptions in Twentieth-Century Writing approaches this dialogue from two interrelated perspectives: it asks how modern authors' appeal to the classical past opens up new readings of their oeuvres and contexts, and it considers how this process in turn renders new insights into the classical world. This two-way perspective offers dynamic and interdisciplinary discussions for readers of Classics and modern literary tradition.

Fellini's Eternal Rome, Alessandro Carrera
Virginia Woolf's Greek Tragedy, Nancy Worman

James Joyce and Classical Modernism

Leah Culligan Flack

BLOOMSBURY ACADEMIC
LONDON • NEW YORK • OXFORD • NEW DELHI • SYDNEY

BLOOMSBURY ACADEMIC
Bloomsbury Publishing Plc
50 Bedford Square, London, WC1B 3DP, UK
1385 Broadway, New York, NY 10018, USA
29 Earlsfort Terrace, Dublin 2, Ireland

BLOOMSBURY, BLOOMSBURY ACADEMIC and the Diana logo
are trademarks of Bloomsbury Publishing Plc

First published in Great Britain 2020
Paperback edition first published 2021

Cover design: Terry Woodley
Cover image © Irish novelist and poet James Joyce,1882–1941, Zurich, Switzerland, circa
1918. Photo by C. Ruf/Archive Photos/Getty Images

A catalogue record for this book is available from the British Library.

A catalog record for this book is available from the Library of Congress.

ISBN: HB: 978-1-3500-0408-5
PB: 978-1-3501-9370-3
ePDF: 978-1-3500-0412-2
eBook: 978-1-3500-0411-5

Series: Classical Receptions in Twentieth-Century Writing

Typeset by RefineCatch Limited, Bungay, Suffolk

To find out more about our authors and books visit
www.bloomsbury.com and sign up for our newsletters.

For Lucy, Owen, Katie, Caroline, Jack, and Kate, with love
and
For English majors, with gratitude

In loving memory of Steven Wells Flack (1943–2019)

Contents

Series Editor Preface

The present volume marks the third innovative contribution to the series *Classical Receptions in Twentieth-Century Writing* (*CRTW*), a project that seeks to explore the modalities and textures of modern classicisms in the works of writers recognized for their global impact on modern poetics, philosophy, politics and the arts. *CRTW* approaches this aim from two distinct yet interrelated perspectives: it asks how twentieth-century authors' appeals to the classical past open up new understandings of their oeuvres and contexts, and it considers how this process in turn renders new insights into the classical world. In plotting twentieth-century receptions of Greco-Roman antiquity from this two-way perspective, the series aims to promote dynamic, highly interdisciplinary discussions for readers of Classics and Literary and Classical Studies. Indeed, a key feature of the series is its extensive range and scope. It looks at both Anglophone and non-Anglophone writers from modernities around the globe, as well as writers still or until recently active in their field. Each of these authors is considered primarily as a writer whose interest in antiquity has contributed to a significant revision of aesthetics, philosophical and political thought, identity studies, gender studies, translation studies, visual culture, performance studies, urban studies and cultural criticism, among other areas of knowledge. In this sense, *CRTW* aspires to promote a new intellectual space and critical direction for those producing research on Twentieth-Century Studies with a focus on Classics and vice versa.

The series furthermore aims to re-energize aspects of reception premises and practice. Over the last two decades, Classical Reception has developed broadly into four main fruitful areas of investigation: periods and/or movements (e.g. Humanism; the Enlightenment; the Victorians), media (e.g. film; sculpture; painting; the stage; musicology; comics), theory and criticism (e.g. psychoanalysis; gender studies; deconstruction; postcolonialism); and geopolitical regions (e.g. Africa; the Caribbean; Latin America; Eastern Europe; Australasia). These lines of enquiry have been instrumental in shaping methodological agenda and directions, as well as offering tremendous insights into discourses of Greco-Roman antiquity in space and time. Yet, within the histories of classical receptions focusing on periods and regions, the twentieth century has been underexamined as a thematic unit. On the one hand, there has been a preponderance of focus on studies in English on Anglophone, Francophone and Germanophone receptions. This has been in part corrected by postcolonial reception studies with a focus on geopolitical regions outside of Western Europe. What has been missing is a perspective that combines not only an appreciation of non-Western receptions, but also an understanding of these reception phenomena within a global, and not merely regional, framework. *CRTW* seeks to address this tangible gap, moving beyond isolated treatments and into full-scale investigations of authors recognized both for radical re-readings of the classical past and for challenging received ideas about the identity and cultural mobility of antiquity in the Western tradition. Interdisciplinarity is at the heart of such a reconsideration of reception in the series. Instead of treating reception as a sub-discipline of Classics, or as an expansion of the disciplinary boundaries of Classics, *CRTW* conceives reception as a hub for interdisciplinary exchange among multiple subjects, disciplinary practices and scholarly expertise. It addresses some of the most profound shifts in practices of reading, writing, and thinking in recent years within the arts and humanities, as well as in the poetics of reading the classics that one finds in twentieth-century writing itself.

Beyond reception, each individual study in the series draws attention to the specific quality of a modern author's classicism, as well as the various ways in which that author negotiates classical ideals and values typically found in, for instance, early twentieth-century Ireland. Such is the case with James Joyce's transformative reading of the classics in his experimental fiction. In *James Joyce and Classical Modernism*, Leah Culligan Flack offers a new way of conceiving the role of the classical in the author's engagement with antiquity, from his early works to the publication of *Ulysses* in 1922. Instead of concentrating on how Joyce attempts to break with the classics, Flack draws attention to a continuity between his classical learning and modernist aesthetics, arguing that classics and his modernism are inseparable categories, since the classics are precisely what furnish the language of the "new" in his oeuvre, as well as the vehicle that informs his defiant attitude towards the status quo of his time. Examples of this inflexion in Joyce's classical modernism form the body of Flack's thought-provoking study. In her close readings of *Dubliners*, *Stephen Hero*, *Portrait*, and *Ulysses*, she illustrates how Joyce creates an "illicit" form of classicism, which she brilliantly calls "cloacal", and which involves the "expression of the vulgar and the bodily processes that famously offended Joyce's readers". In her exploration of Latin-based "classical passwords," Flack shows how Joyce exploits this device in his works to speak "illicitly" against pedagogical, social, religious, sexual, and political convention (Chapter 1). So does Joyce appeal to his knowledge of Greek and Roman history to criticize the "heroic ideology, nostalgia, and logic of violent martyrdom" that feeds and sustains Irish history and subject formation (Chapter 2). Flack's study furthermore focuses on how Joyce's classical aesthetics in turn invites us to consider new forms of reading the interplay between the *Odyssey* and *Ulysses*. Moving away from criticism that plots Homer's epic as a model for Joyce's novel, she develops a comparative approach to the two texts, highlighting their unique self-reflexive character and akin attitude towards art and life, the act of reading, the nature of audiences, and the Western tradition (Chapter 3). Alternative forms of reception of Joyce are the central subject of Flack's closing chapter. Here, she introduces two contemporary literary responses to the author: Alison Bechdel's *Fun House* (2006) and Maya Lang's *The Sixteenth of June* (2014), both of which continue to pursue questions that preoccupy Joyce in his fiction, such as whether and how to read the classics in the modern world. Both titles also encourage readers to consider the value of institutionalized academic readings of the author, especially in the case of readers who are after a more personal connection with his oeuvre. Flack's most important conclusion is that these texts promote new "radically personal models of reading, including partial readings and mis-readings" that recuperate the worth of individual acts of reception in defiance of academic authority. This is, most likely, a strategy of reading Joyce and his courageous approach to the classics and his world that Joyce himself would have approved.

Laura Jansen
University of Bristol

Acknowledgments

While working on this book, I have been reminded of all of the ways that stories can save us and have saved me. Although I did not intend to write a book solely devoted to Joyce after I finished my first book (*Modernism and Homer*), I am grateful that Laura Jansen contacted me to ask me if I would be interested in this project. Given how much I had to narrow my focus on Joyce last time, I was excited by the possibility of having more space to pursue the vast subject of Joyce and the classics, even knowing I would still not be able to be anything close to comprehensive.

I did not realize that this would be exactly the book I needed to write in a period of personal and cultural uncertainty. Retracing Joyce's way of reading the classics helped me to inhabit his courageous worldview, his belief in the possibilities of what literature might accomplish, and his ability to take seriously the power of the imagination to keep the possible in view as possible. I needed all of these things as I worked on this project. I am grateful.

I thank Laura and the entire editorial team at Bloomsbury, including Lily MacMahon, Emma Payne, and Alice Wright. My experience working with them has been unusually wonderful because of their professionalism and commitment. I am also grateful to the external readers for helping me to recognize big and small things about this project with fresh eyes.

Each week, I find myself feeling grateful for English and humanities majors everywhere—for young people who continue to make a commitment to asking questions, thinking independently, communicating with precision, and cultivating the imagination. I consider myself so lucky to work with the fantastic undergraduate and graduate students at Marquette who have shared their creativity, their imaginations, and their truest selves with me as we have talked about Joyce, Dostoevsky, and many others. The literature classroom remains my favorite place because of them. In particular, as I have worked on this book, I have been heartened by the passion, intelligence, and commitment of my students, Danielle Clapham, Jackielee Derks, Jessie Wirkus Haynes, Max Patchet, and Katherine Stein.

At this stage in my career, I am lucky to have the support and encouragement of many brilliant friends working in my fields. Anne Fogarty and Bridget Murnaghan have been there as invaluable sources of support at key moments in my career—they both helped me to feel as though I belonged in this profession while I was a junior scholar who did not quite believe that yet. Kris Ratcliffe fundamentally reshaped the trajectory of my own narratives about my life, and I will be forever in her debt. In the Joyce world, Vicki Mahaffey, Sean Latham, Stephanie Nelson, Claire Culleton, Michael Patrick Gillespie, Richard Rankin Russell, Paige Reynolds, Luca Crispi, Sophie Corser, and Greg Baker have been wonderful interlocutors. I thank my friends, the brilliant scholars Sarah Keller and Celia Marshik for their support and camaraderie. As someone crossing fields, I am grateful to have learned so much from talking with and engaging with the inspiring work of Marianne Hopman, Emily Greenwood, Justine McConnell, David Scourfield, Elizabeth Vandiver, and Alison Rosenblitt. In particular, the third chapter of this book comes from discussions I had with Marianne a decade ago. At the time, I could not imagine how to write a chapter like this. While writing the third chapter, I was delighted to discover the difference a decade has made. Marianne's influence remains in it, and I thank her.

I am lucky to have talented and supportive colleagues at Marquette. I have learned so much working and teaching alongside my colleagues in the English department. I give special thanks to Al Rivero, John Su, and Gerry Canavan for their mentorship and support as I worked on this project. I have also been lucky enough to develop a supportive network of friends across campus and thank Jeanne Hossenlopp, Christine Hill, Jennica Webster, Allie Hyngstrom, Kati Berg, Cindy Petrites, Amber Wichowsky, and John Borg for their collegiality and support. Special thanks go to Gary Meyer for his strong support and transformative mentorship of me as I worked on this project.

Finally, I thank my family and friends for their love and support. I remain deeply grateful for Matt Flack, who has helped me maintain the energy I needed to write this book and who has always supported me. I am a better person because of him, and I thank him. I also promise him to talk about James Joyce a little less from now on. Melissa and Kyle Haak have shared all of the big moments of my life for more than three decades, and I thank them for being my chosen family. Amy Jo Wozniak helped Milwaukee to become my home, and I could not have finished this project without her love, friendship, support, and humor. She knew what 2018 could be before I did. Mike Rinaldi remains my personal survival guide and is the first person I will call in the case of a natural disaster or, more likely, a small disaster, like a nine-pound dog getting stung by a bee. I also remain grateful for Kristen Tripp Kelley, Ray Kelley, Rebecca Joslin, Laurie Kohler and many other friends who have filled my life with laughter and light.

I am thankful for Peg Flack and Erin Davis for welcoming me into their family with such generosity and love. Nancy Ferranti, Pat Graml, and Rich Ferranti have been there for me whenever I needed the wisdom of (young!) elders, and it has meant so much to me to know they are there. Mike and Julie Culligan have been steadfast in their support and love.

This project has been marked by my gratitude for those who mentored me and my awareness of my commitment to my children and to the children of my heart, my nieces and nephew.

I dedicate this book to the memory of Steve Flack, who passed away as I was in the final stages of completing it. I thank him for his wisdom and for going out of his way to accept me and love me and my family. I will never forget him.

I have also dedicated this book to my children, Lucy and Owen, because their courage and joy have helped me maintain hope and perspective. They give my life and my work meaning. Lucy is one of the best writers I know. Her strength in the past few years encouraged me to be a better person. She also has reminded me each day of how important it is to remain actively grateful for all that is good. Owen may be a budding Joycean. When I went through what I imagine may be a common Joycean experience of trying to figure out the best word to use to describe Joyce's description of Bloom looking at the backside of the Venus statue to check out its anatomical accuracy, I decided that a five-year-old was probably the best expert I might consult on this matter. I asked Owen the question and waited in suspense. Finally, he simply responded with two terms I had never heard him (or anyone) use: "That's easy. Just call the poop tube the butt finale." Tempted as I was, I went in another direction in Chapter 3, but I am glad I could find room for his contributions here. On the off chance that my dog learns to read before this book comes out—Ernie, thank you for your patience. I will be available for more walks soon.

My life has been enriched by the bountiful spirit and love of Jack and Kate Davis. I am grateful for each of them and have taken great joy in seeing them become the strong, kind, thoughtful people that they are. Caroline Culligan has taught me for her whole life about fierce individuality and kindness, and one of the greatest joys of my life has been watching her turn into the talented, strong person she is—capable, wise, self-possessed. Katie Culligan has turned out to be either my secret twin or spirit animal (or both). She is the English major and fiercely original, brilliant writer to whom I also dedicate this book, with love.

Abbreviations

CW	Joyce, James. *The Critical Writings*. Edited by Ellsworth Mason and Richard Ellmann. New York: Viking Press, 1959.
D	Joyce, James. *Dubliners*. New York: Norton, 2006.
FH	Bechdel, Alison. *Fun Home: A Family Tragicomic*. Wilmington: Mariner Books, 2006.
JJ	Ellmann, Richard. *James Joyce*. Oxford: Oxford University Press, 1983.
L	James Joyce, *Letters*, vol I, II, III. Edited by Richard Ellmann. New York: Viking Press, 1966.
O	Homer, *The Odyssey*. Translated by Emily Wilson. New York: Norton, 2018.
P	Joyce, James. *A Portrait of the Artist as a Young Man*. Edited by Jean Paul Riquelme. New York: Norton, 2007.
SH	Joyce, James. *Stephen Hero*. New York: New Directions, 1963.
SJ	Lang, Maya. *The Sixteenth of June*. New York: Scribner, 2015.
SL	Joyce, James. *Selected Letters*. Edited by Richard Ellmann. New York: Viking Press, 1957.
U	Joyce, James. *Ulysses*. New York: Vintage Books, 1986.
UA	Don Gifford and Robert Seidman. *Ulysses Annotated*. Berkeley: University of California Press, 1988.

Introduction

Reading and Reception in Joyce's Classical Modernism

In February 1914, *The Egoist* published the first installment of James Joyce's new novel, *A Portrait of the Artist as a Young Man*, which famously begins with a Latin epigraph taken from Ovid's *Metamorphoses*: "*Et ignotas animum dimittit in artes.*"[1] Although many later editions offer a footnote translating this line (for example, the Norton Critical edition translates it as "He turned his mind toward unknown arts"), *The Egoist* did not translate it and therefore created a hierarchy of readership that depended on a knowledge of Latin and of Ovid—knowing readers recognize that Joyce is recruiting Ovid to announce a turn toward unknown arts.[2] Directly following this epigraph is *Portrait*'s innovative opening, which conveys Stephen's experience in a style that approximates the consciousness of a very young child. The classical epigraph and the experimental style collaborate to announce the innovation of the novel that follows—in this moment, the classical serves as a language of the new.

For a century, Joyce has prodded readers to read the classical tradition in new ways, in part because of the significant role he understood that reading might have as a personally and socially transformative experience. On October 14, 1921, he wrote from Paris to his aunt Josephine Murray in Dublin and told her, "If you want to read *Ulysses*, you had better first get or borrow from the library a translation in prose of the *Odyssey* of Homer" (*SL* 286). Like many of Joyce's later readers, she struggled to make sense of *Ulysses* and gave her copy away, much to her nephew's chagrin. When Murray's daughter Kathleen informed Joyce that her mother thought that *Ulysses* wasn't "fit to read," Joyce replied, "If *Ulysses* isn't fit to read, life isn't fit to live" (*JJ* 537). This sentiment extended his earlier position when a publisher, Grant Richards, refused to publish *Dubliners* without major revisions. Joyce wrote to Richards in 1906, "I believe that in composing my chapter of moral history in exactly the way I have composed it I have taken the first step toward the spiritual liberation of my country" (*SL* 88). He continued, "I seriously believe that you will retard the course of civilization in Ireland by preventing the Irish people from having one good look at themselves in my nicely-polished glass" (*SL* 89–90). These statements reveal an abiding belief in what the process of reading might accomplish individually and socially. Joyce's insistence that his readers read the *Odyssey* together with *Ulysses* offers us a snapshot of the artist urging modern citizens to read to gain the psychological and spiritual freedom that might enable wider forms of political, social, and sexual freedom.

Joyce's fiction treats reading and rewriting the classics as useful, even urgent, activities. Declan Kiberd recently championed this model of reading in an impassioned book that opens with a pair of chapters entitled "How *Ulysses* Didn't Change Our Lives" and "How It Still Might Do So." Kiberd's work attempts to reclaim *Ulysses* for a non-specialized reader by redefining what it means to read Joyce according to the ideas about reading evident in his fiction.[3] As Kiberd understands it, Stephen's students "prefigure a world, our world, in which the steely precision of Latin has declined, only to be replaced by a new priestly discourse of critical jargon."[4] This comparison exposes the intertwined legacies and futures of the study of both classics and Joyce in the twenty-first century.

Ulysses and Us was perfectly timed at the end of the global financial crisis that peaked in 2008, a crisis that led to a swift and as yet unreversed decline in the study of the humanities.[5] The financial crisis coincided with the geographical and temporal expansion of how we define modernism, in a movement dubbed the "new modernist studies" by Douglas Mao and Rebecca Walkowitz.[6] By the time the recession hit, classics as a field had already begun the process of adapting to the changing marketplace of the university, which was most visible in the explosion of interest in classical reception studies. In 2003, Lorna Hardwick sketched out the principal aims and methods of classical reception studies as an alternative to the "classical tradition" approach, which studied "the transmission and dissemination of classical culture through the ages, usually with emphasis on the influence of classical writers, artists, and thinkers on subsequent movements and individual works."[7] She explains that the inadequacy of this approach rests in the narrowness of perspectives it allows;

as an alternative, classical reception studies "have to be concerned with investigating the routes by which a text has moved and the cultural focus which shaped or filtered the ways in which the text was regarded."[8] In 2008, Hardwick collaborated with Christopher Stray to evaluate the evolution of the field and the "so-called 'democratic turn' in classical reception analysis," which foregrounds the expansion of classical knowledge to "less privileged groups" in the modern era, an expansion that might be taken as analogous to the expansion happening at the same moment in modernist studies.[9] The following sample of recent studies in classical receptions affirms the sense Hardwick and Stray articulated about the promise of this new turn: Jennifer Ingleheart, *Masculine Plural: Queer Classics, Sex, and Education* (2018); Fiona Cox, *Ovid's Presence in Contemporary Women's Writing: Strange Monsters* (2018); Melinda Powers, *Diversifying Greek Tragedy on the American Stage* (2018); Brett M. Rogers and Benjamin Eldon Stevens, *Once and Future Antiquities in Science Fiction and Fantasy* (2018); and Edith Hall and Justine McConnell, *Ancient Greek Myth in World Fiction since 1989* (2016).

Joyce is a major stop on the route many texts have traveled from the ancient to the modern worlds, and he helped to initiate the democratic turn that Hardwick and Stray methodologically name as part of their field of study. Until the past few years, classical reception studies has had relatively little to say about modernist writing and has focused more on contemporary and postcolonial receptions, a scarcity Miranda Hickman addresses in the volume co-edited with Lynn Kozak, *The Classics in Modernist Translation* (2019), which identifies classical modernism as an "emergent subfield."[10] Testifying to the relatively recent emergence of studies dedicated to modernism and the classics are Alison Rosenblitt's recent study of E.E. Cummings (*E.E. Cummings' Modernism and the Classics*, 2016); Elizabeth Vandiver's study of the poetry of the First World War (*Stand in the Trench, Achilles*, 2010), as well as her recent work on Richard Aldington; David Scourfield's forthcoming work on Ford Madox Ford, E.M. Forster, and Virginia Woolf; studies of Woolf by Jean Mills (*Virginia Woolf, Jane Ellen Harrison, and the Spirit of Modernist Classicism*, 2014) and Nancy Worman (*Virginia Woolf's Greek Tragedy*, 2018); and, in Joyce studies, Randall Pogorzelski's study, *Virgil and Joyce: Nationalism and Imperialism in the* Aeneid *and* Ulysses (2016). My 2015 book, *Modernism and Homer*, consciously avoided placing Joyce at the center of modernist classical receptions and read the "Cyclops" episode of *Ulysses* according to paradigms drawn from Ezra Pound, Osip Mandelstam, and H.D. *Modernism and Homer* called for a recalibration of how we understand Joyce—rather than approaching him as the center of a canon from settled points of view, I argued that we need to revisit Joyce as a Catholic writer from a colonized nation who did not approach his work or the classics from a position of settled canonicity and whose works in fact scrutinize the power of the institutions that later championed his work.[11]

Neither that study, nor this one could possibly aim to have the final or definitive word on Joyce and the classics in a longstanding, robust conversation that includes important work by Stuart Gilbert, Hugh Kenner, Michael Seidel, Fritz Senn, W.B. Stanford, R.J. Schork, Stephanie Nelson, Keri Ames, and many others. As I worked on this book, I was reminded of how much I benefited from the century of study that has already been devoted to this issue. I appreciate Schork's reflections on his work in *Latin and Roman Culture in Joyce* in 1997: "no one would deny the essential relevance of these matters to a serious study of the works of James Joyce. But a book on Joyce's use of the languages and literature of ancient Rome? Stuart Gilbert's guide and schemata would seem to have revealed all anyone needs to know about epic analogues for *Ulysses*."[12] Twenty-one years later, these doubts remain. However, my study arises, as Schork's did, from a sense that a century of vigorous discussion about Joyce and the classics has not exhausted the subject and that more remains to be said. More particularly, Joyce offers an essential point of view that should be included in contemporary conversations about classical modernism and about the way forward for classical and literary studies at a moment when various forms of global crisis have raised questions about the value of studying Greek, Latin, or modernism.

Joyce's fiction has influenced our understanding of the position of the classical tradition in contemporary life, in part because it challenges its readers to read against the grain of institutionalized reading practices that deploy classical literature as a means of discipline, regulation, and social legitimation. Seth Schein has described the legitimating function of the classics in the following way: "The power of the 'classical' does not spring, as is usually thought, from its relation to a real or imagined past, but from its relation to current social, political, and moral values that it helps to legitimate."[13] Joyce understood that the classics served as a disciplinary instrument of regulation in turn-of-the-century Ireland, but he also reshaped and remade that tradition so it might serve as an engine of human connection and freedom. As one center of the modernist canon, Joyce's *Ulysses* has become a cultural icon of difficulty sometimes appropriated by a professional class of academic readers whose interpretive practices reinscribe the kinds of institutionally-sanctioned reading practices his fiction challenges. In this study, I return to Joyce's work to examine its vision of the rebellious, empowering potential of the classical tradition for its readers. A diachronic reading shows that Joyce consistently turned to ancient Greek and Roman literature, language, and culture at critical moments in his aesthetic development, not to stabilize his writings, but rather to innovate. As such, I aim to emphasize the classical as central to our sense of the most daring dimensions of his writing.

From the moment I embarked on a project that touches on Joyce, the classics, and modernism—three incredibly complex subjects in isolation that pose obvious challenges when brought together in a single, relatively brief study—I accepted that I would have to make massive omissions to avoid various kinds of intellectual shipwreck. These omissions were, in the end, guided by my selection of a coherent organizing framework that would make visible some of the process by which Joyce arrived at what I take to be his exciting approach to the classics. Stephen Dedalus and prototypes of Stephen in *Dubliners* ended up being the most useful conceptual nucleus for this study. As I suggest, Joyce developed his distinctive perspective on the relationship between the classical and modern worlds in his depictions of classical education within a complex matrix of sociopolitical, religious, and psychological experience. I trace the early evolution of his emerging classical concerns mainly through Stephen's growing awareness of the risks and rewards the classical tradition offered his artistic future. This study, therefore, touches only glancingly on Bloom and Molly, even though much more remains to be said about how these characters fulfill what Stephen is striving for in *Portrait* and *Ulysses*, an enabling relationship to the classical world embedded in the reality of everyday experience. The most significant omission here is a sustained analysis of *Finnegans Wake*. My selection of Stephen as a kind of portal between the classical and modern worlds for Joyce was the first, but not the only, reason for this omission. Joyce's early engagement with the classical world focuses on Greco-Roman culture and culminates in his own participation in the epic tradition of this culture in *Ulysses*. In *Finnegans Wake*, Joyce moves beyond his rewriting of Greco-Roman and Judeo-Christian traditions to think more expansively about universal history. However, this does not mean that the project of *Finnegans Wake* is totally separate from my claims here. I argue that Joyce advocated for a model of classical reading that embraced ambiguity, openness, and multiple meanings. *Finnegans Wake* seems to me to be the culmination of this enterprise. Finally, my argument here hinges on the impact of the classics in the early development of the features of Joyce's aesthetic that we now recognize as modernist. It seems to me, as it has seemed to many other of Joyce's readers, that *Finnegans Wake* marks a new stage in Joyce's aesthetic development, one that is sometimes aligned with the postmodern and that exerted a much narrower influence. Even given the mountain of scholarly texts dedicated to Joyce's use of the classical world, future scholarship will have a lot to add to contemporary classical receptions conversations about how *Finnegans Wake* fulfills the ludic aesthetic toward which his early work is heading.

Joyce and Classical Modernisms

As I worked on this study, the phrase "classical modernism" began to emerge to denote the relationship between the classical tradition and modernism. Joyce's engagement with the classical world in the service of a subversive, experimental aesthetic must be understood as distinctive against the backdrop of his contemporaries in part because the particular valences of literary production associated with Irish modernism are distinct from Anglo-American and continental modernism.[14] Joyce's distance from his fellow modernists becomes apparent when we compare a Joycean definition of modernism to a more generalized definition. In their *A Critical Companion to James Joyce*, A. Nicholas Fargnoli and Michael Patrick Gillespie offer a useful definition of modernism that helps to contextualize Joyce:

> Literary modernism constitutes a movement that interrogates the legitimacy of traditional social institutions such as the family, the church, and the state, rejecting their authority to prescribe and enforce moral standards of behavior. Instead modernism allows individuals, in literary works quite often artists, the right to disregard social norms of unethical conduct. As a

corollary, perhaps, literary modernism (like modernism in other arts) is characterized by formal experimentation, entailing the use of such devices as stream of consciousness, ambiguity, the unreliable narrator and self-reference (the authorial highlighting of the text as fiction), breaking the illusion of verisimilitude. Styles are highly individual, varying greatly from author to author.

Scholars usually place Joyce—along with T.S. Eliot, D.H. Lawrence, and Virginia Woolf—among the foremost proponents of modernism in English. One might certainly argue that *Dubliners* and most certainly *A Portrait of the Artist as a Young Man* fit the modernist mold. However, a great deal of debate has taken place over the issue of whether *Ulysses* is in fact a modernist or a postmodernist work, and most critics feel that *Finnegans Wake* clearly falls into the category of postmodernism.[15]

Compare this Joycean definition to the more general definition of modernism in *The Oxford Dictionary of Literary Terms* (a representative example of more generalist definitions of modernism):

A general term applied retrospectively to the wide range of experimental and avant-garde trends in the literature (and other arts) of the early 20th century, including Symbolism, Futurism, Expressionism, Imagism, Vorticism, Ultraismo, Dada, and Surrealism, along with the innovations of unaffiliated writers. Modernist literature is characterized chiefly by a rejection of 19th-century traditions and of their consensus between author and reader: the conventions of realism, for instance, were abandoned by Franz Kafka and other novelists, and by expressionist drama, while several poets rejected traditional metres in favour of free verse. Modernist writers tended to see themselves as an avant-garde disengaged from bourgeois values, and disturbed their readers by adopting complex and difficult new forms and styles. In fiction, the accepted continuity of chronological development was upset by Joseph Conrad, Marcel Proust, and William Faulkner, while James Joyce and Virginia Woolf attempted new ways of tracing the flow of characters' thoughts in their stream-of-consciousness styles.[16]

This more general definition of modernism focuses on the avant-garde and on the formalist and epistemological innovations of modernist artists and writers. The Joycean definition, however, begins with the idea of social critique—of family, church, state, etc.—before then moving to a tentative assertion that formal experimentation serves the broader social critique of the modernist text.

The significance of this hierarchy for my study is that Joyce's experimentation with classical texts and languages also is inextricably linked to his fiction's analytical scrutiny of nation, empire, gender, class, race, and religion.

As difficult as it is to find a comprehensive literary agenda that could encompass texts as various as *Ulysses, The Waste Land, BLAST, Jacob's Room, Cathay,* and *The Autobiography of Alice B. Toklas,* it is nearly as difficult to articulate a simple agenda that can capture all of Joyce's fiction from *Dubliners* to *Finnegans Wake.* As Michael Levenson points out, Joyce's career follows the trajectory of modernism itself from the "small self-contained unit—the Image, the epiphany, the short story—toward ambitious, sometimes sprawling, works of synthesis."[17] By the time Joyce wrote *Ulysses,* he was committed, if anything, to a program of ongoing stylistic experimentation that resists generating or relying on its own paradigms. In *Ulysses,* he identified his objective as "writing a book from eighteen different points of view and in as many styles, all apparently unknown or undiscovered by my fellow tradesmen" (*Letters* I 167).[18]

The past forty years have marked a shift in how we read Joyce, with critics such as Emer Nolan, Andrew Gibson, Luke Gibbons, Vincent Cheng, Seamus Deane, and others putting Joyce's engagement with Irish politics and history back into the conversation. In broad strokes, as we became more aware of the political, psychosexual, cultural dimensions of his writing, there was no going back to a purely formalist sense of Joyce as a modernist innovator devoid of national or social context. As Stephen Dedalus declares his intention to remain "elusive of social orders," so too Joyce has remained elusive of literary orders, fitting in many literary categories, but none perfectly (this sample of book titles gives us a sense of this: *Semicolonial Joyce, James Joyce and the Mythology of Modernism, James Joyce and Modernism, The Illicit Joyce of Postmodernism, Modernism and Postmodernism in Joyce's Fiction*). Despite the inevitable evasiveness of this term, I nevertheless keep it in view because the classics are implicated across the twentieth century in attempts to identify the modernist qualities of Joyce's writing.[19]

Joyce's incompatibility with his contemporaries can be glimpsed in the 1914 volume of *The Egoist* that launched *Portrait.* Running alongside *Portrait* were some of H.D.'s best-known Imagist poems, including "Hermes of the Ways," "Incantation (Artemis over the body of Orion)," and "Oread," exemplars of her hallmark style in the era, which was marked by classical allusions, verbal economy, and sculptural precision. The issues of *The Egoist* that ran installments of *Portrait* also contained a number of translations and critical pieces about Greek and Roman culture, including a translation of Remy de Gourmont's "The Horse of Diomedes" and Richard Aldington's enthusiastic critical response to de Gourmont's *Le Latin Mystique*, which helped Aldington to defend his notion of the classics as a protection against the ills of modernity. "For the barbarous days draw near to us," he writes, "and soon you will seek from Cornwall to Sutherlandshire and find no books save novels and scientific tracts; the word 'Greek' is already a reproach, and literature is in the hands of the dull and degreed or the avaricious or the duped and degraded devotees of singularity."[20] Aldington later bemoans the "anti-Hellenism" of contemporary writing and hopes for a return to the beautiful simplicity of Greek writing, so much so that he concludes that "modern artists might produce a few good works of art if they looked at it with the kind of feeling . . . Plato had when he composed the short poem spoken by Socrates."[21] Aldington's view stems from his interest in the classical world offering a standard and a perspective to be imitated by modern artists.

This number of *The Egoist* also included alongside Aldington's piece "A Curious History," the account of Joyce's extensive struggles against various forms of censorship to publish *Dubliners*. This juxtaposition perfectly foregrounds Joyce's attention to the particular publication conditions that shaped reception by actual twentieth-century audiences. Joyce's reading of ancient Greek and Rome always kept plainly in view the material and historical conditions of the text, which is illustrated most clearly in the 1934 Random House publication of *Ulysses*. A new reader facing the novel's title would have turned first not to anything obviously having to do with the classics, but rather to Judge Woolsey's landmark decision that *Ulysses* was not pornographic, a letter from Joyce about his battles with censors, and a foreword about this history by Morris Ernst.[22] The material text makes plain the interconnection between the scandalous and classical elements embedded in the experience of reading it.

Joyce's work has had a polarizing influence on readerly communities for a century. An early review of *Portrait* by Diego Angeli called it a "cry of revolt" and concluded that Joyce is "a new writer with a new form of his own and new aims, and he comes at a moment when the world is making a new social ordinance. We must welcome him with joy. He is one of those rude craftsmen who open up paths whereon many will yet follow. It is the first streaks of the dawn of a new art visible on the horizon. Let us hail it therefore as the herald of a new day."[23] However, many of Joyce's contemporaries rejected significant aspects of his writing, either for reasons of form or more often for the apparent vulgarity of his work (which annoyed or offended even some of his most enthusiastic readers, including Pound). Many were offended by what H.G. Wells called the "cloacal obsession" of his writing, an element a later reviewer succinctly identified when he called Joyce "a perverted lunatic who has made a speciality of the literature of the latrine."[24] Some readers also rejected the seeming incoherence of *Portrait*. In a reader's report for Duckworth and Company, Edward Garnett called the novel "too discursive, formless, unrestrained" and concluded that it was "too unconventional." Joyce's relationship with the classical tradition emerged as a critical issue through which critics could engage in a debate by proxy about the value of his work. Aldington responded to the serial publication of *Ulysses* by writing, "Mr. Joyce with his great undisciplined talent is more dangerous than a shipload of Dadaistes."[25] T.S. Eliot entered the conversation with the influential essay "Ulysses, Order, and Myth," which refuted Aldington's claim that Joyce was a "prophet of chaos." In response, Eliot proposed the influential concept of Joyce's mythic method, which involves "manipulating a continuous parallel between contemporaneity and antiquity" as a way of "controlling, of ordering, of giving a shape and a significance to the immense panorama of futility and anarchy which is contemporary history."[26] Aldington later wrote to Eliot that his article was fallible, but that he remained concerned that Joyce's influence would lead incoherence to be mistaken for genius. He concludes that what modern art needs is a "classic style—sobriety, precision, concision—is and must be the most beautiful thing in literature and all deviations from it must be retrogression."[27]

Many responses to Joyce share a presumption that the classics mattered primarily as a compositional tool and an aesthetic standard. When we speak of classical modernism—loosely defined as the network of influential modernist texts that depend in significant ways on establishing a relationship to the classical past—it is important to remain alert that there were in fact different versions in the teens and twenties, not all of which were compatible with one another. I employ the phrase "classical modernism" in relation to Joyce's work to underscore the fact that Joyce's classicism cannot be separated from the features of his work that might be called modernist (e.g. stylistic experimentation, social critique and rebellion, psychological portraiture). The classical world animated his defiant, innovative creativity in a way that helped him to develop his ideas about reading.

From the beginning of his career through *Ulysses*, Joyce relied on the classical tradition as a laboratory of modernist innovation that helped him to conceptualize the most shocking and vulgar dimensions of his writing. The classical world did not serve as a distant aesthetic standard or as a corrective to the chaos of modernity. Rejecting the notion of a classical tradition as static and distant, Joyce's work is interested in its circulation and operation in modern social structures, in the modern political imagination, and in the modern mind. In what follows, I track the development of Joyce's classical modernism from *Dubliners* through *Ulysses* to consider how he has taught and might continue to teach us to read classical texts as rebellious, unstable, and indeterminate. As such, I will argue that his work offers us an alternative critical lineage to twentieth-century views of the *Odyssey*, in particular, as a source of Eliotic mythic order or what Erich Auerbach in his description of the *Odyssey* calls "fully externalized description, uniform illumination, uninterrupted connection, free expression, all events in the foreground, displaying unmistakable meanings, few elements of historical development and of psychological perspective."[28] One of the reasons why ancient Roman and Greek culture served Joyce so well over the long trajectory of his career is because he read the *Odyssey* and the classical world more generally as rife with ambiguity, contradiction, openness, and possibility. His reading more closely resembled other turn-of-the-century readings of Homer by critics such as J.A. Symonds and J.P. Mahaffy, who tended to read classical literature as "thoroughly modern, more modern even than the epochs quite proximate to our own,"[29] and by readers such as Oscar Wilde, who admired the subtlety and nuance of Homer's psychological portraits of women in the *Odyssey*.[30]

Joyce's Classical Readers

Joyce's fiction shows an evolution of a subversive, rebellious deployment of classical languages, texts, and figures that consolidate an exclusive interpretive community defined not by class or nation but rather by engagement with verbal play and textual difficulty. Just as his schoolboy characters speak dog Latin to one another to evade easy detection by outsider listeners in positions of power, Joyce reshapes the classics into a playful language of rebellion accessible only to readers willing to accept the investment his works require. Whereas the majority of other writers working in English in the high modernist period used the classics from a writerly perspective, he approached ancient Greek and Roman culture as an archive of complexity that helped him conceptualize what the process of reading might entail and what it might accomplish.

Joyce's fiction is populated by a diverse range of moments of private and collective reading (which includes misreading and partial reading, among others). These show the text anticipating the various interpretive moves readers might make, including deploying classical words—what I call in Chapter 1 classical passwords—as red herrings that seem to offer interpretive shorthands. One of the key classical passwords of *Ulysses*, "metempsychosis," illustrates the versatility of the text's anticipation of the ways readers might respond to such interpretive prompts.[31] *Ulysses* introduces "metempsychosis" in "Calypso" in the first conversation of the day between Bloom and Molly. Molly is reading *Ruby: Pride of the Ring*, a text that might not obviously require annotation and glossing, and she asks Bloom for the meaning of the word. As Hugh Kenner argues, Joyce changed the name of *Ruby: A Novel Founded on the Life of a Circus Girl* to enhance the potential ambiguity of the title (by leaving open whether the ring was jewelry or a circus ring) because "he never tired of devising small illustrations of the extent to which understanding relies on context."[32] In their discussion, Molly and Bloom reproduce the pedagogical exchange so familiar throughout Joyce's works, with Molly in the position of the student and Bloom in the position of the classical pedagogue:

> —Show here, she said. I put a mark in it. There's a word I wanted to ask you.
> She swallowed a draught of tea from her cup held by nothandle and, having wiped her fingertips smartly on the blanket, began to search the text with the hairpin till she reached the word.
> —Met him what? he asked.
> —Here, she said. What does that mean?
> He leaned downward and read near her polished thumbnail.

—Metempsychosis?

—Yes. Who's he when he's at home?

—Metempsychosis, he said, frowning. It's Greek: from the Greek. That means the transmigration of souls.

—O, rocks! she said. Tell us in plain words.

(*U* 4.331–42)

Molly and Bloom here perform different kinds of responses to trying to define "metempsychosis." Bloom's definition is insufficient for Molly in part because she perceives that his answer generates additional semantic and contextual complexity without answering what she takes to be her straightforward question. He internally considers how to formulate a better response and unintentionally crafts the neologism "metamspychosis," which suggests and enacts the mutability of the word even as he attempts to gloss it for her. He proceeds to define it ("Reincarnation: that's the word") and offer examples before they are both distracted by the smell of the kidney he left on the stove (*U* 4.351, 4.361). There is no evidence that this pedagogical exchange did anything to clarify *Ruby: the Pride of the Ring*—in fact, as Mary Power has shown, the word "metempsychosis" does not appear in Amy Reade's 1889 novel (*UA* 78). Molly's question sends Bloom to other contexts to try to define and explain the classical word, and it sends Joyce's readers on a fruitless quest to the intertext. Bloom's failure to confirm Molly's understanding coincides with the failure of Joyce's classical passwords to "tell" in "plain words" what *Ulysses* means. This pedagogical scene is framed by this kind of failure.

Nevertheless, "metempsychosis" has served as a useful pedagogical and critical anchor for readers' guides and classrooms attempting to put together a coherent critical framework to ease the task of reading Joyce's novel for the first time. In his full-length study of *Ulysses* (which was available before the international ban on *Ulysses* was lifted), Stuart Gilbert justifies the kind of attentive reading *Ulysses* demands: "It is possible to read *Ulysses* as most of us read the book of life, uncritically, forgetfully, following the line of least resistance; and though a greater vigilance would afford a richer pleasure in perusal, the casual reader will reap a reward proportionate to his effort."[33] Gilbert begins his reading of "metempsychosis," for example, by calling it "one of the directive themes of the work."[34] He moves from the first reference to "metempsychosis" in "Calypso" back into readings of esoteric texts and

Viconian philosophy in the context of their significance not only to *Ulysses* but also to *Finnegans Wake*. This reading amplifies the miniature internal reading Bloom performs and suggests that the Greek word initiates a multifaceted cross-textual reading process that rewards readerly ambition and creativity while generating (and insisting upon) interpretive openness.

However, if we take Molly's request for "plain words" as emblematic of the kind of process first-time readers undergo when they attempt to answer many of the novel's classical questions, starting with the one evoked by its title, then we notice that this kind of request goes unanswered by both Bloom and Gilbert. Critics of *Ulysses* have rejected what Leo Bersani calls the "affectless busyness" of this kind of a readerly process that "invites intertextual elucidations as a strategy to prohibit textual interpretations."[35] Leonard Diepeeven points out more generally of modernist writing that the experience of recognizing allusions was both "too much in the foreground and too simple an activity" that creates a "reading experience that was not rich but impoverished."[36] Kiberd's work analyzes the process by which "... *Ulysses* was wrenched out of the hands of the common reader. Why? Because of the rise of specialists prepared to devote years to the study of its secret codes—*parallax, indeterminacy, consciousness-time* being among the buzz words ... In doing this, they have often removed Joyce from the Irish context which gave his work so much of its meaning and value."[37] From different angles, these critics have underlined a problem that has undermined the notion of a wide readership for classical modernism in the twenty-first century. And, in different ways, they identify Joyce's classical passwords and the modes of specialized reading they invite as part of the problem.

Joyce's deployment of terms such as "metempsychosis" offers an alternative view, one that emphasizes the potential for classical words and texts to form bonds precisely because they are not bearers of static, official meanings. At the end of *Ulysses*, Molly remembers Bloom's lesson when she thinks about the time when he lost his job at Hely's: "and I was selling the clothes and strumming in the coffee palace would I be like that bath of the nymph with my hair down yes only shes younger or Im a little like that dirty bitch in that Spanish photo he has nymphs used they go about like that I asked him about her and that word met something with hoses in it and he came out with some jawbreakers about the incarnation he never can explain a thing simply the way a body can understand" (*U* 18.561–7). Her reflections here reject Bloom's explanation but reveal the intimate nature of their bond. She thinks of the same images he thought of, but did not speak, as he attempted to posit an explanation when he noticed *The Bath of the Nymph* and thought, "Not unlike her with her hair down: slimmer" (*U* 4.371). By the end of the day, the word itself has been utterly transformed into "met him pike hoses," a password that speaks to her connection to Bloom, "who has also internalized this error."[38] This pedagogical error acquires a life of its own across the span of the novel, most notably in "Eumaeus" and "Ithaca." The fatigued "Eumaeus" narrator notes that Bloom "then recollected the morning littered bed et cetera and the book about Ruby with met him pike hoses (*sic*) in it" (*U* 16.1472–3). The intrusion of "sic" here suggests a pedantic underscoring of a classical error in a way that is at odds with the syntactic imprecision of the rest of the sentence—this kind of correction ironizes the logic that demands classical precision, the kind of logic associated with the Jesuit teachers who play such a prominent role in Joyce's early fiction. In "Ithaca," the narrative voice enumerates Bloom's catalogue of "instances of deficient mental development in his wife" and concludes with the following: "Unusual polysyllables of foreign origin she interpreted phonetically or by false analogy or by both: metempsychosis (met him pike hoses)" (*U* 17.485–6). As Kenner points out, "Parallax falsifies"—Bloom adds his own error to Molly's list of mental deficiencies which he keeps in order to preserve his sense of pedagogical utility in their home, and he and Molly share a false memory of a Greek word that has been transformed into an inaccurate approximation of its sounds. "Met him pike hoses" is "metempsychosis" misread and misremembered, and it self-consciously enacts the theory of metempsychosis in the novel. In so doing, it overthrows pedantic approaches to classical languages and articulates a ludic classical model grounded in shared values of imprecision, transformation, and human connection.

Redefining the Classical

The fact that the moment is ripe for renewed conversation between classicists and modernists may be attributed in some measure to the important work in classical reception studies that has recognized the function of errors in

modernist classical texts. This recognition prompts us to rethink earlier
negative characterizations of modernist writing by classical scholars charging
modernist texts such as Pound's "Homage to Sextus Propertius" with ignorance
of classical languages and traditions. Hickman notes this change in the
introduction to *The Classics in Modernist Translation*:

> Yet recent work has begun to turn such views around: the modernists are
> increasingly credited (to adapt Carne-Ross's formulation) as progressive
> poet-translators who deliberately transformed the classical work they
> engaged and pursued translation as both a critical and creative mode. As
> Vandiver observes here, modernist work with classical materials was often
> based in critique of what the moderns saw as pedantry; our volume stresses
> that what were once perceived as modernist failings born of ignorance or
> irresponsibility are now often seen as deliberate departures from traditional
> scholarly methods, aimed to "make it new."[39]

As such, we are prepared to reopen a conversation that has been somewhat
dormant in recent decades about Joyce's classical interventions. Rather than
being an attack on the classics, Joyce's work emerges from an increasingly
visible sense of the classics as a tool of rebellion against convention. Rather
than being a carrier of socially-affirmed meaning attesting to shared values in
a community, Joyce's classical writings tend toward ambiguity, antagonism,
and the illicit. Therefore, one reason why we cannot call upon a static sense of
the classical to describe Joyce's fiction rests in the fact that early on, he himself
abandoned this kind of notion and embraced a more unsettled model of what
and how the classics might mean in the twentieth century.

Joyce's fiction shows the process by which he eventually abandoned a
version of the classical that was more in sync with his modernist contemporaries.
As Theodore Ziolkowski notes, there are two separate prevailing uses of these
terms in relation to early twentieth-century art, the first of which very generally
refers to ancient Greek and Roman culture. The second use recruits the classical
as the epitome of "the values of simplicity and order" in modern art.[40] This
kind of classical aesthetic served as a guiding principle of the movement
anticipated by T.E. Hulme in his 1912 essay "Romanticism and Classicism," in
which he foretold the coming of a period of "dry, hard, classical verse" defined
by verbal precision and what Ezra Pound would call in his Imagist manifesto
the "direct treatment of the thing" (a rejection of both Romantic and Symbolist

modes of representation).[41] This aesthetic culminated in the early poetry of the Imagists, particularly H.D., whose work Pound championed as "straight talk, straight as the Greek!"[42]

In *Stephen Hero*, Stephen's aesthetic theories rely on this kind of classicism. Unique to this text, among all of Joyce's fiction, are Stephen's extended conversations about how to define the classical and modern in relation to one another. *Stephen Hero* makes clear that his definition of the classical is not tied to any historical period, as he insists to the college President that Aeschylus is not a classical writer. Elsewhere, he attempts to define ancient art spatially, not temporally, as "meaning art between the Balkans and the Morea" (*SH* 33). The conversation with the President shows the importance Stephen places on defining his terms as well as his struggle to do so, with Stephen arguing:

> — But the Greek drama is heroic, monstruous. [sic] Eschylus is not a classical writer!
> — I told you you were a paradoxist, Mr Daedalus. You wish to upset centuries of literary criticism by a brilliant turn of speech, by a paradox.
> — I use the word "classical" in a certain sense, with a certain definite meaning, that is all.
> — But you cannot use any terminology you like.
> — I have not changed the terms. I have explained them. By "classical," I mean the slow elaborative patience of the art of satisfaction. The heroic, the fabulous, I call romantic. Menander perhaps, I don't know . . .
> — All the world recognises Eschylus as a supreme classical dramatist.
> — O, the world of professors whom he helps to feed . . .
>
> (*SH* 97)

Stephen here is committed to definitional clarity as he develops his aesthetic principles. The President points out at the conclusion of this conversation that he finds Stephen's theory "a little juvenile," but admits that he has been very interested by it. He foretells that Stephen will one day mature and amend his theory when his "mind has undergone a course of . . . regular . . . training and [he has] a larger, wider sense of . . . comparison . . ." (*SH* 98; ellipses in original).

Between *Stephen Hero* and *Portrait*, Stephen and Joyce seem to have undergone precisely the kind of development the President predicted. In fact, there is no attempt in *Portrait* to define the classical or the modern, a topic that preoccupied *Stephen Hero* and the writings of Hulme, Pound, and Aldington in the same period. A quick search of both works affirms this change. *Stephen Hero* uses the word "classical" seventeen times, the word "ancient" sixteen times, and the word "modern" twenty-seven times (and this frequency of course, represents only the part of the draft that is extant). *Portrait* uses the word "classical" once, "ancient" twice, and "modern" twice, and none of these descriptors are used to give voice to Stephen's aesthetic viewpoint. In fact, the one time the word "classical" appears in *Portrait*, it is used by Donovan at the culmination of him bragging about his academic accomplishments to Stephen and Lynch and his condescending insistence that as a member of the field club, he is a "highly respectable" person. He ends by asserting the classical as a sign of his intellectual and class status by saying to Stephen and Lynch, "Goethe and Lessing ... have written a lot on that subject, the classical school and the romantic school and all that" (*P* 186). Stephen says nothing in response and, when Donovan departs, Stephen tells Lynch that this statement reminds him of how he responded to Donovan bragging about the field club: by calling after him that he should bring him some turnips. Not only does Stephen not talk about the classical and modern, as he did in *Stephen Hero*, he is dismissive to the point of being contemptuous of those who do, in part because of the social context in which notions of the classical are bandied about. Far from being an abstract aesthetic ideal, Joyce's sense of the classical was consistently and inextricably enmeshed within the fabric of the social, cultural, and political dimensions of lived experience. This material sense of the classical emerged from and is indebted to his academic experiences in Irish Jesuit schools.

As a student at Clongowes Wood College, Belvedere College, and University College Dublin, Joyce was immersed in a classical tradition shaped by Jesuit pedagogy during a moment of educational transformation. The Intermediate Education Act, which passed in 1878, a few years before Joyce's birth, set standards for a new form of compulsory rote education and fact-based learning. As Bruce Bradley observes, Clongowes Wood College was a hub of conflict after this Act's passage, because many of the Jesuit educators there still followed the 1599 *Ratio Studiorum*, the humanistic model of Jesuit pedagogy.[43] Years after its passage, in the 1911 *Studies in the History of Classical Teaching*, Rev. T. Corcoran, S.J. cites a seventeenth-century book by William Bathe, which argues for a moral dimension of studying classics and laments that the rote learning that followed from the Intermediate Education Act had replaced the role of the classics to enhance students' ability of "self-expression."[44] More than a century earlier, Richard and Maria Edgeworth, describing classical education as "toil and misery," reflected on the limitations of classical education, which aimed not to enable students to speak or read Greek but rather to know enough to impress their contemporaries.[45]

As Schork explains, Greek and Latin carry oppositional meanings in Joyce's fiction in ways that can be traced back to ways sectarian division shaped classical education in Ireland.[46] Latin was the premiere classical language taught in Ireland and on the continent and as such, it served as a signal of class status and cultivation. Joyce's academic records show his very high levels of success in his study of Latin (against the backdrop of his mediocre performance in general). He never studied or became fluent in reading Greek, though his working notebooks for *Ulysses* and *Finnegans* Wake show his use of Greek dictionaries and his interest in etymology. In the memorable opening scene of *Ulysses*, Buck Mulligan occupies a position of social condescension to Stephen that stems from his British education at Trinity and Oxford, where Greek was the mark of cultural power (as part of the aptly named "Greats" curriculum).[47] This condescension is most visible when Buck tells Stephen, "*Epi oinopa ponton*. Ah, Dedalus, the Greeks! I must teach you. You must read them in the original. *Thalatta! Thalatta!* She is our great sweet mother" (*U* 1.78–80).[48] This Greek Homeric quotation here does not merely serve to reinforce the novel's Homeric affiliation—more importantly in this moment, Buck wields Homeric Greek as a signifier of his cultural superiority over Stephen, one that is reinforced by imperial domination as realized in the British educational system. Likewise, Stephen's commitment to Latin goes beyond scholastic interest in the ancient world; his association with Latin signifies either his parochialism (from Buck's perspective) or his linguistic resistance to English domination.[49] This exchange, then, puts Homeric language at the center of a symbolic conflict between competing classical ideologies and an actual political conflict between colonizer and colonized.

Joyce's early fiction does not merely allude to the classical—it depicts the operation of classical values as a means of social control in the particular context of turn-of-the-century Ireland under the control of the British Empire and the Roman Catholic Church. His representations of classical education as a disciplinary mechanism fit within a much broader international history of classical education. In her study of the history of Latin, Francoise Waquet notes that by the eighteenth century, discussions of Latin tended to center upon "a sort of moral and intellectual efficacy that Latin—or at least its study—were claimed to possess."[50] Strikingly, she shows how little this conversation changed between the eighteenth century and 1924, when the American Classical League listed the objectives of classical education, which included: the "development of correct mental habits"; the "development of an historical and cultural background"; and the "development of right attitudes toward social situations."[51] If, as Waquet's study shows, Latin was essential in the formation of a civilized man in the eighteenth and nineteenth centuries, it made a fitting target for Joyce's analytic scrutiny. It also offered him a versatile resource for consolidating a community of rebellious critique.

Chapter Overviews

To clarify the ways that Joyce's classical modernism anticipates the formation of Joycean interpretive communities, Chapter 1 examines the depiction of classical education in *Dubliners*, *Stephen Hero*, *Portrait*, and *Ulysses*. Taken together, these works suggest that Joyce created an illicit form of classicism, which I call cloacal classicism, which rewrites the classical as an expression of the illicit, the vulgar, and the bodily processes that famously offended Joyce's readers. Most of Joyce's first readers did not know what to do with his fiction's tendency to depict bodily processes and other material realities often excluded from notions of the literary.[52] The classical and what we might call the cloacal have usually existed as counterpoints in Joyce's work, the first mediating the distaste caused by the second. Chapter 1 argues that Joyce's early fiction displays the process by which illicit interpretive communities form around what I call classical passwords. Joyce's depiction of classical education seizes control of the classics from his Jesuit masters to express his refusal of their psychological and social power.

Chapter 2 examines Joyce's engagement with ancient history and historiography as he attempted to develop an enabling mode of historical imagination to be realized in his fiction. Joyce's early fiction through *Portrait* shows the ways that children absorb various historical models that become central to their identity. In *Portrait*, young Stephen finds the courage to protest his abuse by the prefect of studies by thinking of himself as one of the great men in Roman history. By the end of *Ulysses*, Stephen asks Bloom to take away a butter knife because it reminds him of Roman history. Between these moments, history is a nightmare for him because he has fashioned himself according to its logic. Greek and Roman history are useful in Joyce's fiction because they serve as an arena in which he can work out the conflicts about the vicissitudes of Irish and European history that shape his life in Ireland and Europe. Extending Robert Spoo's readings of the significance of Joyce's period living in Rome, I show the evolution of a historiographic approach that culminates in a temporary, partial state of detachment, disavowal, and apathy. From a position of historical apathy in "Eumaeus," Stephen can confront history without being destroyed by it.

Chapter 3 returns to a century-old question, the relation between the *Odyssey* and *Ulysses,* to consider how reading the extreme self-reflexivity of both the ancient and modern works alongside one another helps us to better understand a defense of poems, poetry, and literature at the core of Western civilization. Rather than reading the *Odyssey* as a resource that clarifies *Ulysses*, I will use one of the paradigmatic modernist qualities of *Ulysses*—its extreme self-consciousness—to consider what a modernist *Odyssey* might look like. To make this clear, I will focus on what I take to be the most self-reflexive moments in each work: Odysseus's encounter with Demodocus and the Phaeacians on Scheria and the discussion of literature in the library in the "Scylla and Charybdis" episode of *Ulysses*. This connection that I draw is not arbitrary— the only two named references to Homer in *Ulysses* both occur in "Scylla and Charybdis," and one of them features a Revivalist Theosophist extolling the lives of Homer's Phaeacians. Both the *Odyssey* and *Ulysses* depict the dangers of stasis and stagnation and instruct readers toward interpretive agility. To create a personally and socially transformative literature, Joyce reactivates the *Odyssey*'s own presentation of its power to undercut political and gender polarities. More particularly, I argue that Joyce's engagement with women in the *Odyssey* helps him to deconstruct static classical images and ideas circulating in the modern imagination.

The epilogue proposes that contemporary literary responses to Joyce offer new ways of thinking about the relationship between Joyce's work and the classical world.[53] These works, I argue, recover Joyce's way of reading the classics, and they fundamentally disagree with many of the main lines of academic readings that have shaped conversations about Joyce for the past century. I examine Joyce's legacy in a pair of contemporary texts: Maya Lang's *The Sixteenth of June* and Bechdel's *Fun Home*. Both texts lean on Joyce in significant ways in their narrative structures, but both also prominently feature readers who cannot and do not want to read *Ulysses*. Bechdel and Lang keep alive a conversation Joyce's fiction shaped about whether and how to read the classics in the modern world, and in different ways they evaluate why institutionalized academic approaches to Joyce have been unsatisfying to readers seeking personal connections with texts. They promote radically personal models of reading that emphasize the significance of the individual interaction with the text as meaningful.

Joyce's fiction is the perfect interlocutor for Bechdel, Lang, and other modern writers because it accommodates a dizzying range of reading strategies, from the most exacting formalist or historicist interpretations through paying tribute to *Ulysses* by re-enacting it, even if the book itself remains unfinished. The fact that modern citizens can inhabit *Ulysses* becomes visible each year on Bloomsday, when readers from around the world converge on Joyce's lost city, their copies of *Ulysses* in hand, translated into several languages, to participate in a communal experience that is primarily identificatory and affective. Commenting on Bloomsday on Broadway, Robert Fagles noted his pleasure in the "back and forth" reading of Joyce and Homer in the day's "marathon reading" and concluded, "It was Homer and Joyce as I always hoped to hear them: as the two comrades-in-arms they really are."[54] This annual celebration reminds us of Joyce's sense of the power of the classical tradition, which remains alive and well, to serve as a vehicle of human connection and joy.

1

Joyce's Classical Passwords

In 1894–5, James Joyce and J.F. Byrne studied Latin in Father William Henry's class at Belvedere College. Both Byrne and Father Henry ended up playing significant roles in Joyce's fiction—Byrne is the biographical basis of Stephen's friend Cranly in A *Portrait of the Artist as a Young Man* and *Ulysses*. Although Byrne dismissed his Belvedere teachers as being undeserving "of a high rating as a teacher," Father Henry made a stronger impression on Joyce[1]— he appears as Father Butler in "An Encounter" and as the unnamed rector in *Portrait* as the "representative of the powers which threaten to swallow Stephen's individuality."[2] In Father Henry's Latin course, Joyce and Byrne translated Julius Caesar's *de Bello Gallico V*, which appears at multiple pressure points in Joyce's fiction. It also played a surprising role in Byrne's future in a way that sheds light on the formative role of the classics in modernist innovation.

In 1918, two years after Joyce published *Portrait*, Byrne developed what he called the Chaocipher, a dynamic algorithm that he hoped eventually to sell to the US military. Over the years, he tried to lure code breakers and cryptologists into solving his Chaocipher. His most extensive attempt was his 1953 memoir, *Silent Years: An Autobiography with Memoirs of James Joyce and Our Ireland*, which was marketed as a reflection on his relationship with Joyce. However, the true ambition of the memoir becomes plain in its final chapters, which explain the history of the Chaocipher and offer a series of exhibits as examples. In his introduction to the Chaocipher, Byrne had, he notes, "discovered a method of doing something to the written word, in any language, which affected that written word so as to result in its chaotic disruption."[3] In a term that might be applied to Joyce's late modernist work, particularly in *Ulysses* and *Finnegans Wake*, Byrne designated his cipher as the "chaotification of language."[4] He boasts that

In two respects my method for achieving the complete annihilation of order and design in written language is more noteworthy than the method for the disruption of the atom. First, because my method for splitting the word is so simple that it could be performed by any normal ten-year-old school child, and second, because, unlike any other process of explosion or disruption, my method of disrupting the written words is identical and simultaneous with the complete restoration of order and design in the same written words.[5]

Echoing Eliot's description of Joyce's mythical method as a "scientific discovery," Byrne describes his method as both a disruption and a restoration of linguistic order and design.[6] This code achieved a fundamental human ambition: to write a message "in such a way as to be wholly unintelligible to anyone except the person or persons to whom these thoughts were intended to be exclusively addressed."[7] The problem for Byrne was, no one ever solved his code, and the US military repeatedly declined to purchase his Chaocipher.

In the final years of his life, Byrne used his history with Joyce as a kind of lure to entice Joyce's readers into trying to crack his code. His book ends with examples of the code—including a coded version of the Latin *de Bello Gallico*— and a promise of a $5,000 cash prize to anyone who solved it. In January 1947, he described his project to Constantine Curran in the following way: "I am doing a book, largely reminiscent, and including something about Jim Joyce. But the one real purpose I have in writing the book is to make one last effort to 'put over' my cipher system which I invented twenty-eight years ago."[8] One early reviewer picked up on Byrne's intent and argued, "[h]e did see Joyce plain, but he keeps blocking the reader's view of him, although the block maybe is as interesting as the view."[9] Taking Byrne's work alongside Joyce's reveals a curious byproduct of the classical education they both received—the disciplinary structure of institutional Latin propelled both toward becoming authors of classical codes that communities of code breakers, a century later, continue trying to solve. Joyce's modernist writing and Byrne's cipher emerge as different types of modernist classical codes.

As Byrne did, Joyce returns to his classical education to show the process by which he arrived at his own form of linguistic "chaotification." Joyce's scenes of classical pedagogy show how and why he arrived at the radical verbal and stylistic experimentation that is central to what we understand to be his particular brand of modernist innovation, one that depends on the classical tradition to enact both a disruption and a restoration of order. Joyce's early scenes of classical learning show that his turn toward a modernist aesthetic was not an inevitability but rather resulted from an ongoing, intensive engagement with classical languages, literature, and culture and from his reaction to the enforcers of classical knowledge in modern Ireland, which he associated with the Catholic Church, the British Empire, and a repressive, disciplinary contemporary Irish society. Tracking Joyce's depiction of classical education and his strategic deployment of Latin and Greek in his early fiction reveals the essential role the classical tradition played in his creation of an artistic agenda defined by aesthetic complexity, stylistic experimentation, and social rebellion.

Joyce's fictional depictions of the classical pedagogical relationship anticipate the ways that the classical world offers a set of passwords that form interpretive communities in his era and our own. Joyce's depiction of the disciplinary exclusivity of the classics may be viewed as part of a larger cultural trend in the nineteenth and twentieth centuries, where increasing social mobility endowed the classics, which had long served as a symbol of social status, with increased value for an aspirant class. Samuel Johnson identified this commodification of the classics when he wrote, "Greek ... is like lace; every man gets as much of it as he can."[10] Joyce's use of classical allusion subversively extends a process Kenneth Haynes identifies as central to the cultural deployment of allusions in Victorian literature, which serve as "passwords, code phrases, shibboleths to assert one's membership in the class of gentlemen."[11] As Paul Valéry noted of his classical education, "we only develop that which (according to the conventions) identifies a class and that which enables us to move and navigate within a restricted circle—as *passwords*, for Greek and Latin are no more than passwords. There's no question of actually knowing them."[12] Rather than demanding knowledge as a prerequisite to assert one's class status, Joyce's allusions seem to have the opposite effect: they demand that readers manage and respond to ambiguity and uncertainty. Joyce's classical allusions serve as passwords that have the effect of creating a readerly community by inviting, if not demanding, a reading process that depends on both responding to open-ended classical riddles and engaging in dialogue with other readers about persistently indeterminate solutions. Although some readers have postulated that this indeterminacy signals Joyce's deferral of meaning to a later, better audience, I agree with John Nash, that Joyce's work addresses the problem of specific, local, contemporary audiences throughout his work.[13] Extending Nash's work to include Joyce's reading and deployment of classics suggests that Joyce's classical enigmas anticipated and scrutinized the reading practices of local, contemporary audiences.

Joyce's scenes of classical education and representations of Jesuit Latin teachers scrutinize a system in which classical languages are passwords testifying to obedience to the edicts of a Roman Catholic community dominated by the British Empire. In what follows, I am interested in the ways in which Joyce's early writings subversively reconfigure classical passwords to construct a community of rebellious critique of Catholic and imperial orders. Joyce's fiction self-consciously depicts the formation of communities who are adept at navigating and deploying classical passwords as an expression of shared values. A resistance to closed, imposed value systems unites this interpretive community. As such, it anticipates its own reception. Consciously or not, twenty-first century Joyceans perpetuate Joyce's classical passwords— students in courses studying *Ulysses* quickly become aware of their presence when they are instructed to read "Telemachus," open their copy of *Ulysses*, and see no such chapter heading. By the end of their study of the novel, they demonstrate their fluency in this system of classical passwords by finishing not chapter 18 of Joyce's novel, but rather "Penelope."

Mimicry, Laughter, and Joyce's Jesuits

Joyce's scenes of classical pedagogy evaluate classical pedagogy as a framework for forming communities around a shared recognition of mutually repressed, transgressive knowledge. An anecdote from his schooldays illustrates this process. In January 1898, the fifteen-year-old Joyce was cast in the role of a schoolmaster in F. Anstey's *Vice Versa* at Belvedere College. Deviating from his scripted role, he seized his moment on stage to burlesque Father William Henry, his Latin teacher. As Joyce's classmate recalled, "he carried on, often for five minutes at a time, with the pet sayings of the Rector, imitating his gestures and mannerisms."[14] For example, Father Henry frequently called out students who could not confidently answer Roman history questions by name and made them stand. Joyce's impersonation overshadowed the play—his classmates, his castmates, and even Father Henry all "received the performance with hysterical glee."[15] This schoolboy performance illustrates Joyce's playfully subversive approach to his classical education—the performance of *Vice Versa* offered Joyce the occasion to inhabit and subvert the position of his Jesuit teacher in order to generate a kind of rebellious laughter that cut across power differences to unite his audience.

Joyce's imitation of his teacher falls under the heading of what R.J. Schork has called "the parser's revenge." As Schork observes, Joyce spent much of his career thumbing his nose at the kinds of expertise enforced by his Catholic Latin teachers and he used his art to enact revenge:

> A parser exacts his retribution when he is able to manipulate his use of Latin so well that even those with some facility in the ancient tongue begin to suspect that the arcane grammar and syntax are being cleverly turned against them. What was, in the classroom, touted as the linguistic instrument of logic has been transformed, in the artist's forge, into a medium of subterfuge, burlesque and adroit vocabulary or structural legerdemain.[16]

This process of transformation is one crucial part of the radical and influential experimentation that defines Joyce's art more generally. This process is not revenge for its own sake, a settling of scores years after the fact. Rather, his fiction suggests that subterfuge and manipulation could in fact erode power hierarchies to form communities of critique. Joyce's readers join his classmates in a kind of usefully subversive laughter at the figure of the rigid, demanding Latin teacher.

This laughter anticipates the subversive, carnivalesque energy of Joyce's later writing in its engagement with the classics. M.M. Bakhtin's analysis of laughter offers helpful context:

> Laughter has the remarkable power of making an object come up close, of drawing it into a zone of crude contact where one can finger it familiarly on all sides, turn it upside down, inside out, peer at it from above and below, break open its external shell, look into its center, doubt it, take it apart, dismember it, lay it bare and expose it, examine it freely and experiment with it.[17]

Joyce's mimicry and rewriting of the classics enlivens the analytic energy of his writing. Classical education serves as a useful target precisely because it serves as a medium of social, sexual, cultural, and religious regulation and domination. In this system, knowledge of the classics serves as a marker not only of cultural prestige but also of obedience to regulation. When Joyce moves from an analytic evaluation of the classical pedagogical relationship toward using classical figures and languages to subvert the system of regulation structured by that relationship, he moves into a more radically experimental aesthetic.

In *Dubliners* and *A Portrait of the Artist as a Young Man*, Joyce uses the figure of the Jesuit classics teacher to scrutinize both the explicit and latent sociocultural dimensions of the pedagogical relationship. This relationship appears on its surface to demand a mutual and strict disciplinary adherence to Catholic moral and social codes, but it actually unites teacher and student in a barely repressed recognition of various kinds of illicit knowledge. Joyce's fiction begins by using the figure of the priest-pedagogue to establish a fruitful intersection between classical pedagogy and moral transgression: "The Sisters," the first story of *Dubliners*, depicts a child narrator trying to discern the meaning of Father Flynn's death and the unspecified sins that haunted his life. As Vicki Mahaffey notes of both "The Sisters" and "An Encounter," the Jesuit teachers serve as "representatives of cultural authority in general, and cultural education in particular"; together, they become a "unified cultural and patriarchal directive."[18] At the intersection of the classical and Catholic elements of Irish culture, Latin serves as the language of this directive and the priest the locus of its authority. In the 1904 publication of "The Sisters" in *The Irish Homestead*, Joyce noted that Father Flynn "had studied at the college in Rome, and he taught [the narrator] to speak Latin in the Italian way" (*D* 206), but in the 1914 publication, he emphasized Father Flynn's classical authority by noting that he, Flynn, taught the narrator "to pronounce Latin properly" (*D* 6). Between the 1904 and 1914 publications, Joyce also expanded the passage in a way that seems to underscore the ways that the priest's knowledge enables his power. The priest taught the boy about the "catacombs and Napoleon Bonaparte," he explains the meanings of Catholic ritual and garments, and he "amuse[s] himself" by quizzing the boy on mortal and venial sins. However, the priest's teaching does not clarify Catholic ritual for the boy—it actually complicates it, transforming what the boy regarded as "the simplest acts" into "complex and mysterious" gestures only priests could understand and explain (*D* 6). As Joyce structures it, the pedagogical relationship does not appear to be primarily invested in the transfer of knowledge from teacher to student. Rather, the teacher asserts his authority by generating enigmas or, in Father Flynn's case, actually becoming a figure of uneasy mystery. The boy cannot identify the source of his apprehension and projects it onto the priest's body. He registers his discomfort with the priest's smile, which exposed his "big discoloured teeth" and his tongue, which he let "lie upon his lower lip" (*D* 7). Proper Latin pronunciation serves as an ineffective mask for everything that seems unknown and improper about the priest's body and his reputation.

"The Sisters" introduces Joyce's preoccupation with enigmatic priest-pedagogues in his early fiction, seen most prominently in Stephen's extended reflections on his teachers in *A Portrait of the Artist as a Young Man*. For example, after Father Arnall punishes Fleming in Latin class, Stephen thinks:

> Was that a sin for Father Arnall to be in a wax or was he allowed to get into a wax when the boys were idle because that made them study better or was he only letting on to be in a wax? It was because he was allowed because a priest would know what a sin was and would not do it. But if he did it one time by mistake what would he have to do to go to confession?
>
> (*P* 42)

Through this series of questions, Stephen exerts a kind of invisible analytic authority that undermines his teacher's power over him. His pathway to power begins with his internal scrutiny of his Jesuit teachers. This moment constitutes a postscript to the boy's dreams in "The Sisters," when he remembers trying to "extract meaning from [Father Flynn's] unfinished sentences" and envisions Father Flynn confessing his sin to him (*D* 5). The dream inverts their waking relationship—in the absence of the social pedagogical structure of repression, the boy gains moral power.

Joyce's most explicit association between classical education and moral transgression can be seen in "An Encounter," a drama of illicit adventure that is framed as an escape from the space of classical education and the authority of Father Butler (a fictionalization of Father Henry). When Father Butler discovers Leo Dillon with a copy of *The Halfpenny Marvel* during a recitation of a Roman history lesson, the story pits the Jesuit-sponsored power of the classics against imaginative freedom afforded by Leo Dillon's illicit, lowbrow, modern stories of western adventure—the Apache Chief squares off against

Julius Caesar inside the Jesuit classroom.[19] Father Butler conjures the social power of the classics to chide the boys for reading such "wretched stuff" instead of Roman history when he remarks, "I'm surprised at boys like you, educated, reading such stuff. I could understand it if you were ... national school boys," suggesting that classical knowledge serves as a marker of social difference (*D* 12–3).[20]

As Margot Backus and Joseph Valente observe, Father Butler is also here enforcing a "generic and institutional divide" between high and low culture and fails to see that the "*Commentarii de Bello Gallico* and *The Apache Chief* share an imperialistic historical theme with considerable contemporary ideological relevance for the pre-Republican Ireland of his day."[21] As Norris concludes, Butler serves as an authority who regulates the classical canon by effectively forbidding transgressive reading and the transfer of knowledge across history and genre. In this depiction, classical education would seem to be merely a mechanism of control to be rebelled against and escaped. However, Father Butler's power to contain his students' "spirit of unruliness" is temporary—as soon as the narrator is away from the "restraining influence" of school, he longs for adventure and for transgression. And, in his distance from his Latin classroom, he realizes that his escape might form a prelude for a more radical form of exile, as "real adventures ... do not happen to people who remain at home: they must be sought abroad" (*D* 13).

The fact that the boys' day of "mitching" culminates with their encounter with the pederast, the "queer old josser," affirms, from one angle, that the flight from the classics classroom is a flight from heteronormative regulation into an illicit form of homosocial and homosexual knowledge that the narrator ultimately represses (*D* 13,18). However, the encounter itself undermines this opposition by suggesting that, in fact, the narrator and josser do not constitute an alternative to but rather reproduce the pedagogical scene. As Margot Backus and Joseph Valente argue, Joyce's depictions of the classroom draw our attention to the "homoeroticized domination and submission that circulate within elite British public schools but also a variant of this economy among Irish Catholic schoolboys," that maps sexual shame and ethnic shame onto one another.[22] The boys' encounter with the josser reveals the extent to which the classical education of elite schools teaches its students to internalize this homoerotic economy of domination and submission.

Structurally, the boys' encounter with the josser re-enacts the exchange in the classroom between Father Butler and Leo Dillon: the josser occupies the position of the teacher—he speaks of school and asks the boys if they have read the "poetry of Thomas Moore or the works of Sir Walter Scott and Lord Lytton," an interrogation not unlike Father Butler asking Leo Dillon if he has read his Roman history (*D* 17). The narrator's education has taught him to respond by feigning preparation—pretending he has read every work. His response creates the conditions for the josser's manipulation of him for his own erotic gratification. The boy unconsciously associates his encounter with the josser with the pedagogical scene when the josser asks him if Mahony is "whipped often at school." The boy notes, "I was going to reply indignantly that we were not national school boys to be *whipped*, as he called it; but I remained silent" (*D* 19; emphasis in the original). The boy thus internally recites the class snobbery of Father Butler in his response to Leo Dillon's reading of *The Apache Chief* (*D* 13). This repetition suggests the boy's transferal of the ideology from the classics classroom. However, in an inversion of regulation and repression, the josser's erotic monologue silences the normative edict. The classics classroom no longer simply functions as the space of regulation from which the boys must escape—it also provides a blueprint for the transgressive, the illicit, and the homoerotic. The narrator and the stand-in for the priest-pedagogue perform a perverted version of pedagogical interrogation, punishment, and pleasure.

Father Butler's class structurally enables what Norris calls the "bibliophilic seduction of the boy"—both the pedagogical and the perverse encounters depend on what Eve Sedgwick calls "ignorance effects," which requires an "on-going strategic deployment of ignorance and knowledge."[23] Near the end of "An Encounter," the boy involuntarily looks at the josser's face when he describes the pleasure of physical beatings, and he meets the gaze of a "pair of bottlegreen eyes peering at [him] from under a twitching forehead" (*D* 19). This moment is the culmination of the boy's earlier examination of the faces of the foreign sailors on the ferry "to see had any of them green eyes for [he] had some confused notion ..." (*D* 16; ellipsis in the original). The ellipsis here opens space for speculation, leaving open the possibility that the green eyes signal foreignness, Irishness, homosexuality, and (via an association with the green carnations that Oscar Wilde wore as a symbol of aestheticism) homoerotic decadence.[24] As Norris argues, "An Encounter" may be read as a "homosexual text simultaneously in and out of the closet," one that evokes a shared recognition of transgressive knowledge.[25] The classical pedagogical relationship facilitates the movement between recognition and repression upon which the story ultimately depends.

A Portrait of the Artist as a Young Man extends this portrayal of the pedagogical relationship generating a mutual recognition and repression of knowledge. As the unnamed director in the vocation scene, Father Henry plays a crucial role in Joyce's declaration of artistic independence in *A Portrait of the Artist as a Young Man,* and he appears to mostly carry over the role of Father Butler into this later work. Early in this exchange, the director makes a casual reference to the robes of the capuchin Franciscans as "les jupes" "up about their knees," which leads Stephen to a series of anxious reflections that transmute the potential for male genital exposure into heterosexual eroticism. Stephen ponders the clothing of women, "their perfume, the feel of a woman's stocking" (*P* 135).[26] Stephen experiences a moment of unacknowledged identification with the director as he "smiled again in answer to the smile which he could not see on the priest's shadowed face, its image or spectre only passing rapidly across his mind as the low discreet accent fell upon his ear" (*P* 135). This exchange precedes the director's call to Stephen to join the order of priests. Even though Stephen relishes the notion that his priestly identity would make him as "sinless as the innocent," he remains erotically transfixed by the possibility that he "would know the sins, the sinful longings and sinful thoughts and sinful acts, of others, hearing them murmured into his ear in the confessional under the shame of a darkened chapel by the lips of women and girls" (*P* 139). Stephen's vision of this future translates the sin of the sexual act into a sinless form of erotic knowledge of the sins of others, toward a form of erotic voyeurism akin to the josser's experience in "An Encounter."

Stephen's projection of himself onto the priest makes possible his escape from this economy of regulation and repression. Crucially, Stephen's decision to reject the director's suggestion that he enter the order depends on his imaginative reflection on other priestly faces that might include his own. After a series of visions of his priestly future, he imagines the words "The Reverend Stephen Dedalus S.J.," and he feels "a mental sensation of an undefined face or a colour of a face . . . Was it the raw reddish glow he had so often seen on wintry mornings on the shaven gills of the priests?" (*P* 141). The repetition of images of priests' faces opens the possibility that the director physically embodies Stephen's potential future. And, as Joyce did when he imaginatively lampooned Father Henry in the school play, Stephen's imaginative imitation of the director liberates him by creating the psychological conditions that enable him to embrace the "disorder, the misrule and confusion of his father's house" over the order of the Jesuits (*P* 142). Joyce's depiction of classical education exposes the process by which he arrives at an aesthetic that depends vitally on both classical order and the disorder it purports to exclude.

Father Conmee's Stroll and the Ironies of Jesuit Latin

The figure of the Jesuit classics teacher appears in *Dubliners*, *Portrait*, and *Ulysses* at moments of aesthetic transition, in a way that suggests that Joyce uses the priest-pedagogue to work out the terms of his narrative and stylistic experiments. "Wandering Rocks," the Cubist collage that serves as an entr'acte between the novel's more stylistically stable first half and its more shockingly experimental second half, illustrates this function of the Jesuit teacher. The opening of "Wandering Rocks" signals a departure from the novel's primary mode of representation, the use of interior monologue, free indirect discourse, and stream of consciousness to depict the experiences of Bloom and Stephen.[27] It also signals a momentary departure from the basic logic of episodic correspondence driving the novel's connection to the *Odyssey*. In the *Odyssey*, Circe tells Odysseus he must choose to travel by the "Rocks Wandering" or past Scylla and Charybdis.[28] As an Odyssean path not taken, this Homeric title underscores the novelty of Joyce's project, his contribution to rather than translation of a tradition initiated by Homer. At this pivot point in the novel's style—at the textual moment when the novel becomes more paradigmatically modernist[29]—Father John Conmee appears. This appearance continues a pattern in Joyce's early fiction where representations of Jesuit teachers appear at points of transition: Father Flynn at the outset of *Dubliners*; Father Arnall at the beginning of *Portrait*, who Stephen claims knows more than Dante because he is a priest; Buck Mulligan at the opening of *Ulysses* as the mock-priest who exclaims to Stephen, "Ah, Dedalus, the Greeks! I must teach you" (*U* 1.79).

Father Conmee was the rector of Clongowes when Joyce was a student, and he is cast, without a name change, in the role of the rector who gives Stephen the impression of justice against Father Dolan at the end of *Portrait*'s first chapter.

As Trevor Williams argues, "Conmeeism," the style used to depict Conmee's inner life, is a "public style, and expressive of the power that Conmee represents in Dublin. Whereas for Bloom a gap exists between his inner and his outer life . . . for Conmee the gap does not seem to exist."[30] Following Williams' logic, the operation of Latin in Conmee's mind makes visible larger cultural forces at work. This vignette strategically deploys Latin to expose the sociocultural contradictions in the way that the classical and the Catholic collaborate in early twentieth-century Irish life. The vignette begins: "The superior, the very reverend John Conmee S.J. reset his smooth watch in his interior pocket as he came down the presbytery steps. Five to three. Just nice time to walk to Artane. What was that boy's name again? Dignam. Yes. *Vere dignum et iustum est*" (*U* 10.1–4). Conmee's aural association between the name "Dignam" and the Latin "*dignum*" would seem to affirm the Christian intentions of his charitable work. His reading of the Latin Scripture at the end of the vignette further aligns his engagement with Biblical Latin and his activities in Dublin. However, the move away from Dignam's name into a Latin homophone suggests that the classical language opens up a space of intellectual detachment that tempers the extent of his sympathetic feeling for the child who has lost his father. The remainder of the vignette corroborates this suggestion—for example, the one-legged sailor prompts him to think "but not for long, of soldiers and sailors, whose legs had been shot off by cannonballs" (*U* 10.12–13).

At two moments, Conmee interrupts himself with the Latin abbreviation D.V. (*Deo volente*)—the first barely masks his disdain for the "reverend T.R. Green B.A." who "will (D.V.) speak. The incumbent they called him. He felt it incumbent on him to say a few words. But one should be charitable" (*U* 10.69–71). The fact that Conmee thinks in terms of the abbreviation suggests the scripted quality of his condescending view of the non-Catholic minister. Later, Father Conmee's thoughts on African missionary—on the "souls of black and brown and yellow men . . . and the African mission and of the propagation of the faith . . ." (*U* 10.143–5)—expose the imperialist logic of the Church. He reflects, "Those were millions of human souls created by God in His Own likeness to whom the faith had not (D.V.) been brought" (*U* 10.148–50).[31] The literal translation of "D.V." here ("as God wills") threatens to undermine its usage (deriving from James 4:13–17) as a Christian expression of humility in the face of human limitations. Here, the inclusion of D.V. threatens unconsciously to expose a logical fallacy of the white man's Burden—if God had created millions of human souls in "His own likeness," then either there is a flaw in the global operation of faith (if God has willed for millions of people not to have faith) or God has created the conditions for imperial domination. Latin here functions as a versatile characterizing device that exposes the imaginative, psychological, and cultural vocabulary that enables the operation of social and political power by the Catholic Church, even via the "kindly humanist" Conmee, one of its more sympathetic exemplars.[32]

Although Conmee's Latin reveals the vocabulary and logic of Catholicism in relation to empire, it offers a versatile resource to envision alternatives. During his walk, he thinks of the nostalgic book that he published in 1902, *Old Times in the Barony*, which Len Platt calls "a Catholic elegy to Protestant landlordism" that captures a "time before modernity prevailed."[33] By contrast, he also thinks of an unwritten book that might be written about Mary Rochfort, who was married to the first Earl of Belvedere. As Gifford explains, Mary Rochfort's husband wrongly accused her of being unfaithful to him with his brother and blackmailed her into confessing with the promise of a divorce. When she confessed, he retracted his promise and imprisoned her on his estate, where she remained until his death in 1774 (*UA* 263). As Norris points out, he envisions the first sentence of this book: "A listless lady, no more young, walked alone on the shore of lough Ennel, Mary, first countess of Belvedere, listlessly walking in the evening, now startled when an otter plunged" (*U* 10.164–6).[34] This first sentence captures the essence of the book Conmee might write in the literary language that suits his nostalgic worldview. However, Joyce's literary language captures the difficulties such a story might present and the limitations of his language in recording this history. Once his scripted, literary account of Mary Rochfort's story ends, his thoughts turn to the problems in narrating, judging, and evaluating this story:

> Who could know the truth? Not the jealous lord Belvedere and not her confessor if she had not committed adultery fully, *eiaculatio seminis inter vas naturale mulieris*, with her husband's brother? She would half confess if she had not all sinned as women did. Only God knew and she and he, her

husband's brother. Father Conmee thought of that tyrannous incontinence, needed however for man's race on earth, and of the ways of God which were not our ways.

(*U* 10.166–73)

The prevalence of the Loeb Library series when Joyce was writing *Ulysses* (it released a major wave of translations between 1914 and 1918) offers a cultural context for this depiction of Conmee moving into Latin to avoid English vulgarity.[35] In the Loeb translations, obscene material was either omitted or translated into a foreign language—if the text being translated was Greek, then potentially obscene words and phrases were usually translated into Latin. As Philip Lawton's work on the Loeb's expurgation policies shows, in this period, the series tended to employ a strategically evasive approach to translation in a way that divided the Loeb's readership into two audiences: the classically-educated male, who could "cope with the material without being corrupted," and women and children, who would be shielded from the content of the passages by the presence of Latin.[36] For all readers, this translation practice set up Latin embedded within an English text—regardless of whether the Latin was understood—to be inherently associated with obscenity. This context makes possible that Conmee's shift into Latin appears to screen him and the reader while actually underscoring the seemingly obscene content of the phrase; as Richard Brown argues, "part of [Joyce's] artistic intention is to highlight the phrase itself and its implications for the upheaval in contemporary ideas."[37]

Of course, as Brown suggests, Joyce's use of Latin in this sequence does not perfectly align with Conmee's. The priest's Latin signals a range of potentially contradictory intentions—Latin seems to provide a weak alibi for a language that, by highlighting its own transgression, becomes even more illicit than its English equivalent. His unwritten book—one that imaginatively deploys Latin to both conceal and emphasize an illicit response to sex—serves as a useful interlocutor for Joyce's unfolding project in *Ulysses* and his own creative use and abuse of Latin. Joyce's aesthetic strategies, particularly those that depict in vivid detail the psychosexual complexity of his characters' inner lives, enable him to author a drama of infidelity that makes literature out of what Conmee takes to be extra-literary musings. Joyce's Latin here does not serve as a screen or as an alibi, but rather enables analysis of the complex and shifting vocabularies of the intersecting spiritual, physical, psychological, social, and sexual lives of his characters.

Joyce's Cloacal Classicism

Joyce's depictions of Jesuit classics teachers enable his analysis of the complex logic of social repression operating in turn-of-the-century Ireland. The schoolboys in his fiction recognize the potential for Latin as a set of subversive passwords signaling their departure from the repressive edicts of their culture. They also illustrate the intersection between Joyce's depiction of classical education and what H.G. Wells identified as Joyce's "cloacal obsession," his ambition to "bring back into the general picture of life aspects which modern drainage and modern decorum have taken out of ordinary intercourse and conversation."[38] This dimension of Joyce's writing, perhaps more than any other, attracted the notice of his early readers, as seen, for example, in an unsigned review of *Portrait* in 1917, which concluded, "Mr. Joyce is a clever novelist, but we feel he would be really at his best in a treatise on drains."[39]

Joyce's cloacal classicism signals his inversion of the cultural value attached to the classics as a medium of propriety and obedience. The "smugging" incident and its aftermath in *Portrait* perfectly illustrate the schoolboys' subversion of classical pedagogy and their subsequent formation of an exclusive interpretive community aligned against Jesuit pedagogical authority. Early on in *Portrait*, young Stephen tries to understand the other boys' discussion of some other boys caught "smugging" in the school square, a detail critics tend to read as either masturbation or homosexual contact. The ambiguity of this term reproduces in Joyce's reader Stephen's naivete and limits the kind of clarity Stephen or Joyce's reader can achieve through reflection— they share a position of interpreting an unspecified transgression. As Valente points out, when Stephen tries to discern the meaning of "smugging," he instinctively runs through a telling series of homoerotic associations with Simon Moonan and Tusker Boyle that show that he understands at least on an unconscious level the nature of the transgression.[40]

These musings lead Stephen to consider the space of the crime—the square—and the bathroom there, the sounds of water and the "queer smell" of the place (*P* 37). As Valente observes, Stephen's reference to the bathroom and vague reference to it as a space where you went to "'do something' that dares not be named" marks it as a space of "homoerotic potential."[41] The bathroom functions as a site of an alternative, subversive classicism—this may be taken as an image of Joyce's classical modernism, which is illustrated by the graffiti on the bathroom wall:

> And behind the door of one of the closets there was a drawing in red pencil of a bearded man in a Roman dress with a brick in each hand and underneath was the name of the drawing:
>   Balbus was building a wall.
> Some fellows had drawn it there for a cod. It had a funny face but it was very like a man with a beard. And on the wall of another closet there was written in backhand beautiful writing:
>   Julius Caesar wrote *The Calico Belly*.
> Perhaps that was why they were there because it was a place where some fellows wrote things for a cod. But all the same it was queer what Athy said and the way he said it. It was not a cod because they had run away. He looked with others in silence across the playground and began to feel afraid.

This bathroom acts as a carnivalesque space that inverts the authority of the priestly teachers who enforce standards of mastery on their students. The first graffiti image renders comically visual a line from a Latin textbook: "Translate *Balbus murum faciebat*."[42] The graffiti itself is a kind of subversive translation across media that exceeds and resists the function of the schoolroom exercise as a demonstration of knowledge. The Latin translation stages a conflict between two different kinds of authority associated with the schoolmaster and his student. In this case, the graffiti is written in red pencil, the pedagogical instrument of correction; for example, a few scenes later, Mr. Harford travels through the classroom "making little signs in red pencil" to correct the boys' work (*P* 40). The anonymous student seizes the pedagogical instrument and its authority from the classroom for the bathroom and in so doing comically reclaims the institutional power of the classics. This scene anticipates Lynch's confession of writing on the backside of the statue of Aphrodite. Taken together, these scenes recall the story told by Pliny the Elder and Lucian about the young man who fell in love with the Venus of Praxiteles, and who left a stain on the back of her thigh after trying to seduce her.[43] This illicit graffiti participates in a wider tradition of erotic graffiti left by amorous schoolboys.

Balbus is the perfect figure for Joyce's classical modernist graffiti—in Cicero's *Letters to Atticus* (47 BC), he engaged in pleasurable activities (building villas) instead of doing the more serious work of the state. This schoolboy graffiti transforms the textbook line into a near advertisement for malingering. Stephen appreciates the joke but also the fidelity of the drawing for actually looking like a man with a beard.[44] The second instance of graffiti resists the notion of translation by using transliteration to turn the Latin title of Caesar's *Commentaries on the Gallic Wars* into a pun, *The Calico Belly*, in a way that anticipates the sonic playfulness of Joyce's later writing. As I noted at the beginning of this chapter, Joyce's friend Byrne turned *De Bello Gallico* into code to illustrate his Chaocipher. Here, "The Calico Belly" also serves as a kind of code, an in-joke for the schoolboys. In fact, the transliteration itself signals a kind of refusal of the pedagogical process of translation and an alternative approach to understanding the relationship between Latin and English. Though Stephen cannot link the graffiti to the developing scandal at his school, he does have a vague sense of the square as a transgressive space of illicit classical writing.

In this way, the square functions as a formative site in the emergence of what eventually became distinctive as Joyce's classical modernism, which treats the classical world as a medium for a crucial, ongoing power struggle. The classical world did not offer him a field of study through which he could demonstrate his submission to the standards of his teachers and, by extension, the Church. The classical world offered him a series of figures, forms, and verbal codes that he could use to challenge and unsettle the intellectual, spiritual, and psychological power of all of the forces that asked for his submission. Reading this scene in dialogue with an equivalent later scene in the novel brings its formative influence into focus. When visiting Cork with his father, Stephen sees the word "*Foetus* cut several times in the dark stained wood" of the anatomy theater (*P* 78). This word brings to Stephen's mind a vivid image of the schoolboys, the "absent students of the college," that terrifies and disgusts him. Whereas the classical graffiti lured his attention to the schoolboys' erotic knowledge he did not fully understand, the word "foetus" provokes sexual shame in part because he can identify with the schoolboys who carved it. This carved graffiti creates an existential crisis for Stephen, as the "letters cut in the stained wood of the desk stared upon him, mocking his bodily weakness and futile enthusiasms and making him loathe himself for his own mad and filthy orgies" (*P* 80). This moment offers a condensed example of Stephen's agonizing experience of his own biological and familial origins, a problem that haunts him throughout *Portrait* and *Ulysses*. He attempts, but fails, to resolve this crisis on multiple occasions by creating a mythological identity as creator-father and son, Dedalus and Icarus. The square and the anatomy theater create two symbolic experiences where Stephen reads distinct pathways for his future, one grounded in classical play and the other grounded in immutable familial and biological origins.

The square functions as an inversion of the classroom. Immediately after this incident, Father Arnall attempts to reinforce order in Latin class by using the space of classical pedagogy as a space of domination, punishment, and obedience. He scolds his students for their sloppy homework and orders them to write out corrections immediately (*P* 41). He commands Jack Lawton, and then the rest of the class, to decline the noun "*mare.*" When he fails to get beyond the ablative singular, Father Arnall's "face was blacklooking and his eyes were staring though his voice was so quiet" (*P* 41). When Lawton's classmate, Fleming, responds that "*mare*" has no plural, Father Arnall forces him to kneel in the back of the classroom. When the prefect of studies comes in, he beats his hands with a pandybat. The study of Latin becomes an occasion for the enactment of discipline, control, and punishment as a corrective force against sexual transgression. Knowledge of Latin grammar theoretically offers the means for students to demonstrate submission and obedience to the authority of the priest/Latin teacher and the strictly policed heteronormative code he enforces.[45]

Latin, however, also offered Joyce in reality and Stephen in fiction a weapon against pedagogical, social, religious, sexual, and political convention. In *Stephen Hero*, Stephen delivers a controversial essay ("Drama and Life") that makes the case that "[d]rama will be for the future at war with convention, if it is to realize itself truly." This essay is greeted by students and teachers alike as an example of problematic free-thinking. Whelan argues publicly that Stephen has failed to understand "the beauty of Attic theatre"; "Greek art," Whelan concludes, "is not for a time but for all times. It stands aloof, alone. It is imperial, imperious, imperative" (*SH* 101). In this essay, both Joyce and Stephen are rejecting not necessarily Greek art per se, but rather the notion of a timeless and universal sense of the classical tradition. Stephen articulates the need for a truthful, anti-conventional modern form. In this, he is also rejecting the cultural nostalgia of the Irish Revivalists, arguing that "life we must accept as we see it before our eyes, men and women as we meet them in the real world, not as we apprehend them in the world of faery." This point is carried through into *Ulysses*, when Joyce transfers the phrase "imperial, imperious, imperative" to MacHugh, the aging classicist who spends his days malingering in the newspaper offices.[46] MacHugh argues, "We mustn't be led away by words, by sounds of words. We think of Rome, imperial, imperious, imperative" (*U* 7.484–6). He continues: "What was their civilization? Vast, I allow, but vile. *Cloacae*: sewers. [...] The Roman, like the Englishman who follows in his footsteps, brought to every new shore on which he set his foot (on our shore he never set it) only his cloacal obsession. He gazed about him in his toga and he said: *It is meet to be here. Let us construct a watercloset*" (*U* 7.489, 7.491–5). MacHugh offers a comical vision of ancient Rome that actually, from a certain angle, characterizes Joyce's own classical cloacal obsessions, his interest in a mode of classical translation that makes space for what is vile next to what is vast.

In *Stephen Hero*, Stephen's recitation of "Drama and Life" and the argument that follows from it leads to a conversation between Stephen and Cranly in dog Latin, a "language the base of which was Latin and the superstructure of which was composed of Irish, French, and German" (*SH* 106). As Schork points out, this passage and its equivalent in *Portrait* are "Joyce's earliest surviving fragments of original (however corrupt) Latin."[47] Joyce's schoolmate Eugene Sheehy argued that dog Latin may have been "the first intimation of the vocabulary of *Finnegans Wake*."[48] Both Sheehy and Schork sense that Joyce's deployment of dog Latin signifies a moment of innovation. This innovation is defined by an appropriation of an institutional language measured by standards of propriety and exactitude into a playful, idiosyncratic, intentionally erroneous form in a way that reveals that this language's ideology is grounded in error rather than technical proficiency.

Joyce's dog Latin also operates as a miniaturized version of his fiction because it is an exclusive language that consolidates a community around its logic. An event from Joyce's life illustrates this function. In 1902, when Joyce was in Paris, he went to the theater and a brothel and had his photograph taken (the photo is in Ellmann's biography). He had three postcards made and sent one to his family complaining about his lack of money, one to his friend Byrne with a poem on it (*Chamber Music*'s "All day I hear the noise of waters/ making moan"), and one to his friend Cosgrave with a dog Latin poem about French prostitutes. According to Stanislaus Joyce, Byrne was possessive of Joyce's friendship and took pride in being the recipient of this postcard. When he bragged about this to their mutual friend Cosgrave, Cosgrave showed him the dog Latin postcard, which appalled and angered Byrne, both because of its content and because it signified something about Joyce he did not know (which, it seems, was precisely the effect Cosgrave was seeking to have). Stanislaus notes, "At that moment they happened to be passing an underground lavatory," which led Byrne to say, "It's like a thing . . . that a fellow would write down in there, by God."[49] Although Cosgrave says this to wound Byrne, he also articulates the underlying intersection in Joyce's early fiction between his appropriation of classical languages, figures, and texts and his cloacal obsession.

This event in Joyce's life led to his estrangement from Byrne. However, Joyce's fiction recasts this estrangement in multiple ways. In *Stephen Hero*, dog Latin appears to be a private language that reaffirms the intimacy between Byrne and Stephen. After Stephen delivers his lecture, he and Cranly (Byrne's fictional alter-ego) converse in dog Latin, presumably to exclude Madden, who does not speak this language proficiently. Madden, who later becomes Davin in *Portrait*, is proficient in Gaelic, which suggests that dog Latin is an exclusionary alternative to the language of Irish revivalism. Cranly's skill in dog Latin contrasts with his approach to academic Latin—Cranly does not study for his Latin exams, reveals his plan to Stephen to pull out Tacitus as needed to pass the exam, and then he fails to show up for the exam after the first days (*SH* 128–30). In dog Latin, Stephen and Cranly argue about whether Stephen is in a bad mood, and Cranly concludes, "*Credo ut vos sanguinarius mendax estis quia facies vestra mostrat [sic] ut vos in malo humore estis*" (*SH* 106). As Marc Mamigonian and Joel Turner point out in the "Annotations to Stephen Hero," this phrase means, "I believe you are a bloody liar because your face shows that you are in a bad mood."[50] Joyce corrected the "*mostrat*" error in *Portrait*, changing it to "*monstrat*" (*P* 171). In *Stephen Hero*, dog Latin serves as a language of the kind of homosocial privacy made possible by the subversion and redeployment of an institutional language. As Schork points out, Joyce carries this kind of dog Latin into *Ulysses*. In *Oxen of the Sun*, the medicals tell the landlord in dog Latin, "We all will drink the poisonous green, let the devil take our hindmosts."[51] In the 1922 edition, the words are grammatically correct, but in the 1932 edition, Joyce adds an error, changing the correct "*posterior nostra*" to "*posterior nostria*," as Schork notes, "presumably to emphasize the linguistic crudity of both the form and the matter of the saying."[52] Dog Latin offers Joyce a rich verbal field in which he can convey a homosocial bond among men via a strategic and cohering deployment of error.

Joyce's Readers and Classical Enigmas

In 1917, a review of *Portrait* in the *Manchester Guardian* argued, "A little too much is asked of the even eager reader in the way of understanding situations that have not been led up to, and obscure allusions. One has to be of the family, so to speak, to 'catch on.'"[53] This reviewer identified the dimension of exclusivity that *Portrait* and *Ulysses* convey (one could argue that *Finnegans Wake*, which lost many of Joyce's most enthusiastic readers, operates at an even higher degree of exclusivity). Joyce's framing of classical knowledge anticipated these arguments and operated in a way that consolidated communities of critique around classical enigmas and passwords. The cohesion among the schoolboys in *Portrait* around an idiosyncratic use of Latin anticipates the kind of Joycean interpretive communities that have formed in the past century. Classical passwords are perhaps a new reader's first initiation into a reading culture that accepts certain distinctive habits that are part of reading and discussing Joyce. The openings of *Dubliners*, *Portrait*, and *Ulysses* all announce the classical password as the price of admission. As I already noted, *Portrait* begins with an untranslated Latin epigraph—a reader who cannot decode it must choose either to ignore it or to turn to the classical text for answers. The novel's ending's focus on the figure of Dedalus might make readers who chose to ignore the epigraph sense that they have missed something, that they are outside of the novel's epistemological circle. The cover of *Ulysses* invites new readers to keep the classical tradition in view before they open the book—the book's first pages do not fulfill the promise of the title in an explicit way, so new readers are indoctrinated into a process of trying to determine the classical significance of the modern text.

Dubliners did not in its first form begin with a classical password, but the genetic record shows that Joyce added one before the 1914 publication of the text, four months after the serial publication of *Portrait* began. "The Sisters" opens with the unnamed child narrator anticipating the death of Father Flynn:

> There was no hope for him this time: it was the third stroke. Night after night I had passed the house (it was vacation time) and studied the lighted square of window: and night after night I had found it lighted in the same way, faintly and evenly. If he was dead, I thought, I would see the reflection of candles on the darkened blind for I knew that two candles must be set at the head of a corpse. He had often said to me: "I am not long for this world," and I had thought his words idle. Now I knew they were true. Every night as I gazed up at the window I said softly to myself the word *paralysis*. It had always sounded strangely in my ears, like the word *gnomon* in the Euclid and the word *simony* in the Catechism. But now it sounded to me like the name of some maleficent and sinful being. It filled me with fear, and yet I longed to be nearer to it and to look upon its deadly work.

The genetic materials of "The Sisters" show that Joyce made significant changes to the style and substance of this opening between 1904, when he published it in *The Irish Homestead*, and the 1914 publication of *Dubliners*.[54] His changes enhance the ambiguity, allusivity, and psychological portraiture of this scene, and they move the story closer to the aesthetic of *A Portrait of the Artist as a Young Man*, which he was conceptualizing in draft form during these years. His revisions intensify the passage's focus on the boy's inner process of reflection as he tries to determine if Father Flynn has died. His mind eventually settles on the three words that, as many critics note, form a symbolic triad for *Dubliners* as a whole—*paralysis, gnomon*, and *simony*. "Paralysis" helps establish the thematic significance of Dublin as a "center of paralysis," as Joyce famously noted in a letter to his publisher, and "simony" and "gnomon" signal two important forms of knowledge for the young narrator in the catechism and his classical education, which here are associated together in terms of their uneasy and not fully specified power (*SL* 134).[55] The cumulative power of these terms is not fully—or even mostly—in their signification. The act of speaking "paralysis" seems to conjure the other two words and inspire a kind of terrible awe in the boy, who confronts their sound and their association with one another but not necessarily their meaning. Pairing the words "simony" and "gnomon" foregrounds the proximity of the Catholic and the classical in this young mind whose inevitable fate, the collection as a whole suggests, is paralysis.

Euclid's gnomon has offered an interpretive tangle to Joyce's readers, the kind of puzzle Joyceans relish trying to solve. Joyce's Jesuit classical education at Clongowes Wood College, Belvedere College, and University College Dublin offers context for his deployment of this kind of figure. As Thomas Francis Meagher writes, the Jesuits at Clongowes "[t]alked to us about Mount Olympus and the Vale of Tempe; they birched us into a flippant acquaintance with the disreputable gods and goddesses of the golden and heroic ages. They entangled us in Euclid."[56] Meagher's phrasing here reinforces an intersection Joyce also develops in "The Sisters" between the pedagogical classical authority of the Jesuits and the Euclid as a source of intellectual entanglement. The gnomon here does not offer us an interpretive key—rather, it builds symbolic complexity into the story. The gnomon—roughly defined as a large parallelogram with a smaller parallelogram missing from one corner—helps Joyce to project a symbolic logic onto the opening of the story that, as many critics have noted, sets up an interpretive framework for the collection of *Dubliners* as a whole. The gnomon becomes a signal of a new mode of open-ended symbolic reading that Joyce's works will demand.

This classical figure, it should be emphasized, does not resolve the enigmatic nature of the story—it is the expression of the story's puzzle, one that has generated a cacophonous range of readings. Critics have, for example, connected the figure of the gnomon to the elliptical quality of the story, which is riddled with omissions, evasions, and absences—the child narrator attempts to fill in the gaps of what the adults in his life don't say, and readers likewise must infer what is not being said. Drawing on J.E. Cirlot's sense of a gnomon as a "damaged rectangle," Michael Groden reads the gnomon as a figure of irreversible damage—the task of interpretation is not to repair the damage by rendering the figure whole but rather to register the damage and the impossibility of repair.[57] As Groden argues, "Reading is a process of understanding the nature of the wound, the gap, the damage."[58] As he notes,

Joyce's revisions of the text between the 1904 edition and the 1914 edition removed information, which suggests that the gnomon became a symbolic figure of the revised story. Vicki Mahaffey concludes that the gnomic reading process Joyce's story invites calls upon readers to fill in the missing information to complete the figure. Readers can, Mahaffey suggests, fill in the blanks Joyce's story leaves (we can infer, for example, what the silences indicated by the story's many ellipses are communicating). She argues that the next story in the collection, "An Encounter," supplies the information that "The Sisters" withholds and can be used to complete the figure. The gnomon leads both Groden and Mahaffey toward distinct theories of how one might read *Dubliners*—Groden emphasizes recognition as the primary interpretive activity, whereas Mahaffey offers a reading process based in repair and synthesis.

These possibilities, only two among several, suggest that the classical term makes Joyce's work more distinctively ambiguous. Fritz Senn calls for an even more open reading of the figure of the gnomon, which might be viewed not as an incomplete figure, but rather as a surplus figure (with a small parallelogram attached to a larger one). In this context, the gnomon "represents a move, which also happens to be a Joycean proclivity, from the simple toward the intricate."[59] Reading this figure into *Finnegans Wake*, Senn engages in the kind of etymological play Joyce invites and concludes that Euclid (which might etymologically imply "good key," from "*eu*" and "*kleidas*") offers readers a kind of key and a warning about the limits of this kind of reading. As Senn notes, one must "keep in mind that 'me elementator joyclid' (*FW* 302.12) also maintained that 'there is no royal road to geometry.' There we have a key and the assurance that there is no road—as Joycean a constellation as one could want."[60]

I have rehearsed these readings of the gnomon at some length because they illustrate so well the way that Joyce's work—from the first paragraph of his first full-length fictional publication—deploys classical signals to call readers into their positions as co-authors of the meaning of his work. This process of co-authorship sends readers from the classical figure or word in at least two directions—to Joyce's other writings across time and space and to the classical world, language, and cultural context. As the different readings of Groden, Mahaffey, and Senn suggest, the gnomon is more than a figure of classical complexity in Joyce's story—it is also an originating symbol inviting a high-stakes interpretation that might shape how one reads not just "The Sisters" and *Dubliners* but indeed all of Joyce's fiction.

The new mode of reading opened up by the classical figure leads inevitably to social critique. By building the figure of the gnomon into the form of this story, Joyce uses the Euclidean figure in a way that disrupts the stifling power of the priest's mastery of the classical language. He does so by inviting an experience of reading that departs conceptually from the idea of the proper execution of classical knowledge. Rather, Joyce's deployment of the gnomon in his story evokes a playful mode of symbolic reading that depends on epistemological instability and semantic openness. Describing Cixous's approach to "The Sisters," Murray McArthur notes that the story compels a reader into a "double apprenticeship" (Cixous's phrase), "first in the strategic and false mastery of the iconic codes of realist representation and second in the tactical improvisation required by [as Cixous notes,] 'metaphors which never end, hypnotic and unanswerable riddles, a proliferation of false signs, of doors crafted without keys.'"[61] As Cixous and McArthur note, "The Sisters" invites readers to engage in a pseudo-priestly mode of exegesis that is ultimately revealed to be false. By prompting readers toward a mode of "tactical improvisation," "The Sisters" deploys the classical figure to undermine the false mastery embodied by the priest. There is little chance at liberation for any of the characters in "The Sisters," but the story's form enables a mode of psychological liberation by inviting an insistently open-ended mode of interpretation.

Classical errors, as much as if not more than classical knowledge, were incredibly productive for the composition of *Ulysses*. As I discussed in *Modernism and Homer*, Joyce remarked on multiple occasions that "Odysseus" derives from "Outis" plus "Zeus," "Noman-God." This mistake was fortuitous for him, as it helped him to find a classical antecedent for his own model of the sacredness of the everyday. He wrote a variation of this etymology in his notebooks used for language exercises and translations in Zurich in 1918: "outis; oudeis" ("noman; no one") and in the margins "ZEUS." Beneath these entries, he wrote, "NO/GOD."[62] This etymology is wrong—as George Dimock suggests, the etymology of "Odysseus" suggests the dual meaning as one who suffers and causes suffering. In a novel where errors can serve, as Stephen claims, as portals of discovery, it is helpful to recall the etymology of "error" from the Latin meaning "to wander." Joyce's fiction does not invite us to view the classical world as a source of a reassuring sense of order that can help us to manage the complexity of the world he is conveying. The classics do not offer him a set of codes that we can crack—rather, he creates classical passwords that bind his readers to his texts and to one another in communities of open-ended dialogue. His fiction invites us to wander with its characters and through its form on a journey that will not fulfill our desire to be right or to be masters. This wandering shows us, perhaps, that we were always inevitably wrong.

2

"So Let the Ruins Rot": Joyce and Historical Apathy

In October 1906, Joyce wrote to his brother Stanislaus from Rome about his living conditions with his young family. Because his neighborhood's cobbled streets were "fearfully noisy," he jokingly wished they had "buried a few more monarchs or emperors in the neighbourhood" so that the streets would be wooden and therefore quieter. These practical considerations led him to reflect upon what a "fine city" Rome must have been in the "time of Caesar." He concluded, "I wish I knew something of Latin or Roman history. But it's not worth while beginning now. So let the ruins rot" (*L II* 171).[1] This letter illustrates several of the features of Joyce's engagement with history—his topographical interest, his imaginative mapping of the past and present onto one another through his attention to space, his irreverence, and his attention to mundane details.

However, given Joyce's extensive reading of Roman history in school and even at the precise moment when he wrote this letter, when he was reading Guglielmo Ferrero's five-volume history of Rome, it might seem strange that he would disavow his historical knowledge in this way. Yet, this statement is hardly aberrant in Joyce's career. The first mention of Roman history in his fiction, for example, occurs in "An Encounter," as that which the boys do not read (because they prefer Westerns and adventure). Joyce's disavowals shed light on a significant function of Roman history as a field of knowledge where he might work out an apathetic pose that would prove to be useful in his confrontation with Irish history. The end of his 1907 Trieste lecture, "Isle of Saints and Sages,"—which he delivered six months after declaring his wish to "let the ruins rot"—deploys an apathetic tone that refuses the metaphors and ideology of revivalism:

One thing alone seems clear to me. It is well past time for Ireland to have done once and for all with failure. If she is truly capable of reviving, let her awake, or let her cover up her head and lie down decently in her grave forever. "We Irishmen", said Oscar Wilde one day to a friend of mine, "have done nothing, but we are the greatest talkers since the time of the Greeks." But though the Irish are eloquent, a revolution is not made of human breath and compromises. Ireland has already had enough equivocations and misunderstandings. If she wants to put on the play that we have waited for so long, this time let it be whole, and complete, and definitive. But our advice to the Irish producers is the same as that our fathers gave them not so long ago—hurry up! I am sure that I, at least, will never see that curtain go up, because I will have already gone home on the last train.

(CW 174)

This statement issues a muted challenge to the ideology of revivalism that conveys Joyce's physical and psychological detachment from Ireland. The repetition of different forms of the word "let" signals passivity as a response to Irish conflicts about its history in relation to its future. Even if Ireland puts on the play of independence, Joyce does not envision himself as the author of that play, but rather noncommittally says, "let it be whole, and complete, and definitive." He will be neither author nor spectator to Irish independence, which he expresses through his flight from Ireland and from the closing metaphor that suggests that he has already permanently discovered a home in self-imposed exile.

Stephen struggles to adopt this kind of perspective on multiple occasions in *Stephen Hero*, *Portrait*, and *Ulysses*. Even though he is able to open some psychological distance from Irish history, he never fully reaches apathy or disavowal. As Andrew Gibson suggests, the political turn in Joyce criticism reshaped our view of Stephen, which also might reshape our understanding of Stephen's engagement with the ancient past. In place of the disaffected aesthete, readings by Seamus Deane, Vincent Cheng, Len Platt and others presented a view of Stephen as an "aspiring, colonial intellectual and artist whose project—and problem—is precisely independence." *Ulysses* captures Stephen's desperate, failed attempt to arrive at a position of independence via what Robert Spoo calls his "contestatory stance toward history." Spoo argues compellingly that the "persistent historiographic concerns" of *Ulysses* are ultimately Stephen's concerns, even after Stephen "has receded as a character" in the novel's late episodes.[2] I agree with this reading, and I also share Gibson's reading of Stephen's character as dynamic, which can be seen in the complexity of his experience of history over the course of the day.[3] Joyce's letter offers a framework for understanding Stephen's search for independence as a quest to adopt a position of historical apathy, a detached historical vantage point that will create the conditions for his psychological and aesthetic independence.

Joyce's determination to "let the ruins rot" emphasizes his distance from revivalist ideologies that were a dominant force in Irish cultural life at the turn of the century. As Len Platt has argued, *Ulysses* is best understood as being in "precise and explicit antithesis" to revivalist ideology, tropes, and forms.[4] Underscoring the force of Joyce's attack on revivalism, Gibson argues that *Ulysses* is an "historical work that battles fiercely to reverse the emphases of revivalist historiography and reclaim Ireland and its past for Joyce's own culture."[5] Platt argues against viewing Joyce's historiography as a "retreat into mythic historiography or philosophical relativism, or into a sealed world of endless verbal significance, but rather a vital and wildly comic production which is fundamentally engaged with the cultural conditions of its own making."[6] As is evident in *Ulysses*, Greek and Roman history circulate in modern Ireland via the Jesuit educational system to reinforce the value of the ancient past. As Joyce's pedagogical scenes suggest, his Jesuit teachers deployed ancient history as a mark of social status and as an archive of acceptable templates of Irish masculinity by which young boys could fashion their identities. Greek and Roman history emerge as the sites where Stephen and Joyce can work out a model of historical imagination that can oppose the heroic ideology, nostalgia, and logic of violent martyrdom that are central features of revivalism.

Joyce's fiction engages Greek and Roman history to stake out a position of indifference that facilitates a clear-eyed analysis of the nightmare of history. His broadsheet "The Holy Office" articulates the difficulty of actually remaining indifferent: "Where they have couched and crawled and prayed /I stand the self-doomed, unafraid / Unfellowed, friendless and alone / Indifferent as the herring-bone" (*CW* 152). The poem quickly undercuts this professed indifference by concluding, "And though they spurn me from their door / My soul shall spurn them evermore."[7] His address to his literary contemporaries makes plain his commitment to stating his indifference to them and a conflict about the possibility of remaining so. Joyce's fiction illustrates the process by which Stephen engages with ancient history and ancient historians to respond to and then eventually distance himself from the snares of Irish history and of cultural nostalgia.

By mimicking and discarding the logic of the analogy, *Ulysses* challenges the historiographic impulse to view the ancient and modern worlds as analogous. Joyce's decision to remove the Homeric titles from his novel's episodes and thus downplay the analogy usefully illustrates the tension in his work between deploying and abandoning analogies. In a discussion that shows the significance of Standish O'Grady's revivalist historiography as a counterpoint for Joyce's own emerging view of history, Gibson points to O'Grady's insistence on a connection between ancient Greece and ancient Ireland and between himself and Homer. Viewing O'Grady as an interlocutor against which Joyce develops his historiography suggests that the novel's central Homeric analogy actually disrupts cultural links between modern Ireland and the Homeric past.[8] For example, the following "Cyclops" parody scrutinizes the logic of historical analogies:

> A most interesting discussion took place in the ancient hall of *Brian O'Ciarnain's* in *Sraid na Bretaine Bheag*, under the auspices of *Sluagh na h-Eireann*, on the revival of ancient Gaelic sports and the importance of physical culture, as understood in ancient Greece and ancient Rome and ancient Ireland, for the development of the race. The venerable president of the noble order was in the chair and the attendance was of large dimensions. After an instructive discourse by the chairman, a magnificent oration eloquently and forcibly expressed, a most interesting and instructive discussion of the usual high standard of excellence ensued as to the desirability of the revivability of the ancient games and sports of our ancient Panceltic forefathers. The wellknown and highly respected worker in the cause of our old tongue, Mr Joseph M'Carthy Hynes, made an eloquent appeal for the resuscitation of the ancient Gaelic sports and pastimes, practised morning and evening by Finn MacCool, as calculated to revive the best traditions of manly strength and prowess handed down to us from ancient ages.
>
> (*U* 12.897–912)

This parody deploys an overblown style to depict a conversation in Barney Kiernan's pub about Irish revivalism, more specifically the work of the Gaelic

Athletic Association to revive ancient Gaelic sports.[9] Ancient Greece and Rome here appear as cultural exemplars of the ancient world that are used to contextualize and elevate ancient Irish culture and ancient models of Irish masculinity. Joyce uses ancient Greece and Rome to test the meaning and value of the ancient past and to argue against the "desirability of the revivablity" and for letting the ruins of the past rot. For Stephen to strive toward the psychological and spiritual freedom he so desires, but does not achieve, requires him to confront, vanquish, and remake the ancient origins of his modern identity. In this sense, the historiographic work of Joyce's fiction becomes radically personalized as the modern men and women who populate his literary Dublin attempt to become empowered, aware authors of history rather than its helpless subjects.

"The Great Men of History Had Names Like That": Inhabiting Ancient History

Joyce's readings of ancient Roman history as represented in his fiction may be understood in broad strokes as having two stages: childhood, formative readings and mature, analytic readings. As a student at Belvedere College, Joyce excelled in Latin, earning his highest examination marks and winning a Latin composition prize in 1894.[10] Surveying the examination materials on ancient history that Joyce took at Belvedere College, Schork notes both the depth of ancient historical knowledge and the sophistication of historiographic thinking that would have been required of any student.[11] Joyce's degree examinations in Latin at Belvedere College required him to translate not only Horace and Cicero, but also Book XXI of Livy and Sallust's *Jugurtha*.[12] These exams capped a program that included a thorough study of Roman history from the early Republic onward. Known elements of the classical curriculum at Belvedere include *de Bello Gallico V*, Cicero's *De Senectute*, and works by Ovid, Virgil, and Horace.[13]

A recent study of childhood and the classics by Sheila Murnaghan and Deborah H. Roberts helps to contextualize the role ancient history and ancient historical fiction play in the formation of the young Stephen Dedalus and, from what we can tell from available early writings and biographical information, of young Joyce. The nineteenth century saw the emergence of a tradition of literature aimed at bringing classical mythology, literature, and history to an audience of children. To activate a child reader's sense of imaginative wonder, these works depended on an aesthetics of identification and projection so that the ancient historical figure becomes "more than a source of interest to the child reader, he will be the child's self."[14] To develop this idea, Murnaghan and Roberts cite John Stephens' two prescriptive, evaluative criteria for children's historical fiction: "Characters must be credible and invite reader-identification" and "[r]eaders should feel they have learned more about a time and a place through the illusion that they have experienced them vicariously."[15]

Joyce's Jesuit education encouraged him to understand ancient history as a template he might use to fashion his identity. As Bruce Bradley describes, Father Power (the basis of Father Arnall in *Portrait*) divided his class into Roman and Carthaginian teams, thus forcing an historical analogy onto his students by turning his class into a re-enactment of ancient conflict.[16] The first page of *Portrait* displays Stephen's tendency toward an identificatory relationship to narrative—he responds to his father's story of baby tuckoo by concluding, "He was baby tuckoo" (*P* 5).

By all accounts, Joyce launched his writing career by investing contemporary events with classical significance. In 1891, nine-year-old Joyce published his first poem, "Et Tu, Healy," which borrowed the Shakespearean phrase marking Julius Caesar's last words to respond to the death of Parnell. Stanislaus Joyce recalls the poem as

> a diatribe against the supposed traitor, Tim Healy, who had ratted at the bidding of the Catholic bishops and become a virulent enemy of Parnell, and so the piece was an echo of those political rancours that formed the theme of my father's nightly half-drunken rantings to the accompaniment of vigorous table-thumping. I think it was in verse because of the rhythm of bits of it that I remember. One line is a pentameter. At the end of the piece the dead Chief is likened to an eagle, looking down on the grovelling mass of Irish politicians from

> *His quaint-perched aerie on the crags of Time*
> *Where the rude din of this . . . century*
> *Can trouble him no more.*[17]

This poem anticipates Joyce's later widespread use of ancient historical and literary figures to respond to contemporary Irish politics. As a figure who is reminiscent of Rome and of Caesar, Parnell becomes the eagle who has managed to transcend the "rude din" of the century. The figure of Caesar/ Parnell constitutes a potential early avatar for Stephen Dedalus, a classical-contemporary figure who might be part of the conceptual backdrop of his ambition to "fly by" the nets of nationality, language, and religion (*P* 179).

The eagle memorably serves as a symbol of Roman justice in the opening movements of *Portrait*, when the narration of Stephen's early consciousness turns into the emphatic, rhymed, repeated "the eagles will come and pull out his eyes. / *Pull out his eyes, / Apologise, / Apologise, / Pull out his eyes*" (*P* 6). This passage renders ambiguous who is speaking the final rhymed lines.[18] However, Joyce's epiphanies suggest that this voice in earlier form is actually Stephen. This epiphany, Joyce's first, is dated the same year he wrote "Et Tu, Healy" and is structured as a play in miniature:

[Bray: in the parlour of the house in Martello Terrace]
Mr Vance—(*comes in with a stick*) O, you know, he'll have to apologise, Mrs
    Joyce.
Mrs Joyce—O yes … Do you hear that, Jim?
Mr Vance—Or else—if he doesn't—the eagles'll come and pull out his eyes.
Mrs Joyce—O, but I'm sure he will apologise.
Joyce (under the table, to himself)
Pull out his eyes,
Apologise,
Apologise,
Pull out his eyes.
Pull out his eyes,
Apologise,
Apologise,
Pull out his eyes.[19]

This epiphany offers an extremely condensed image of Joyce's early relationship to Roman history. An event rife with sectarian significance he does not understand (his desire to marry Eileen, a Protestant) is filtered through a symbolic framework conditioned by ancient associations, which Joyce then internalizes through repetition and stylizes through rhyme. This insistent repetition stands in contrast to what happened when the young Stephen hears the song about the "wild rose," which empowered him to transform its image (into the "geen wothe") and claim it as his own ("He sang that song. That was his song"). Music and fictional narrative invite the young Stephen to improvise and appropriate, while a historically-inflected sense of justice overpowers him without him being able to reshape it. The nightmare of history that Stephen later names stretches back to the early formation of his consciousness.

The earliest movements of *Portrait* show Stephen taking cues from his culture and envisioning himself according to ancient historical models. When he is wrongly beaten by the prefect of studies for being a "lazy idle loafer" (*P* 43), he filters his anger through a Roman model of justice, prompted by the older boys who describe his condition in Roman terms, telling him, "The senate and the Roman people declared that Dedalus had been wrongly punished" (*P* 46). Convincing himself that the prefect of studies' treatment of him was "unfair and cruel," he engages in historical identification to evaluate his situation, realizing that "A thing like that had been done before by somebody in history, by some great person whose head was in books of history." This act of historical identification leads him to expect justice from the rector, who "would declare that he had been wrongly punished because the senate and the Roman people always declared that the man who did that had been wrongly punished" (*P* 47). These thoughts show the extent to which Stephen has internalized and intensified what the older boys have said, thus making visible the social operation of ancient historical models that he does not fully understand.

Stephen's readings of history strengthen his conclusions about justice and also identification as his primary mode of historical reading:

> Those were the great men whose names were in Richmal Magnall's Questions. History was all about those men and what they did and that was what Peter Parley's Tales about Greece and Rome were all about. Peter Parley himself was on the first page in a picture. There was a road over a heath with grass at the side and little bushes: and Peter Parley had a broad hat like a protestant minister and a big stick and he was walking fast along the road to Greece and Rome.
>
> (*P* 47)[20]

A few mistakes and misunderstandings illustrate the textual origins of Stephen's emerging historiography. First, the misspelling of "Mangnall" signals the approximate, imprecise quality of his memory and his knowledge. As John Simpson points out, Stephen also misremembers the image of Peter Parley—the picture of Peter Parley with a broad hat and a walking stick actually appears in *Tales of Peter Parley about America* (1827).[21] The phrasing of this passage suggests that Stephen seemingly misunderstands the figure of Peter Parley himself, taking a fictionalized speaker (in a book written by Samuel Griswold Goodrich) as the text's author. Although I cannot say with certainty which editions of *Peter Parley's Tales* Joyce read, many of his works do not include the author's name on the title page or, in some cases, anywhere in the book. The revised edition of *Tales of Peter Parley about America* includes an author's foreword identifying the book as his "first adventure in authorship" and reflecting on the fact at the end of his life, he is grateful that his works have earned the favor of children.[22] This foreword is unsigned, thus blurring the boundary between paratext and the text and the author and speaker. Goodrich's text begins with the picture Stephen recalls and the words, "Here I am! My name is Peter Parley: I am an old man. I am very gray and lame. But I have seen a great many things and have had a great many adventures, and I love to talk about them."[23] That misunderstanding changes the meaning of the picture Stephen describes—if Peter Parley were a character, then he would be a fictional persona heading to Rome and Greece to provide a lens through which his young readers could experience Roman and Greek history vicariously. However, by viewing Peter Parley as a real person, the picture captures the textualization of a real person, the author, and his projection into a historical narrative he writes. Joyce's work famously makes use of blurred boundaries between paratext and text, as evidenced by his publication of his early stories under the pseudonym "Stephen Daedalus" and his transformation of this figure into a literary alter ego, Stephen Dedalus.

Peter Parley's Tales offer insight into the structure of ancient historical knowledge that shapes Stephen's approach toward history. *The Tales of Ancient Greece and Rome* treat history and myth as equivalent, starting with tales of Uranus, Jupiter, and the Titans in Chapter 1 before moving into Roman military history in later chapters. Murnaghan notes that this is paradigmatic of the genre of ancient history aimed at children, which "effectively treat[s] myth as part of history."[24] Stephen's reading of this kind of blending of myth and history offers a conceptual backdrop to what he thinks he is doing at the end of *Portrait*, when he mythically refashions himself in order to strive toward historical change (by "forg[ing] in the smithy of [his] soul the uncreated conscience of [his] race" [*P* 224]). Stephen is able to follow the script his education gave him because he has internalized it.

As Sullivan notes, the preface of *Tales about Ancient Rome* explains the author's strategy of using "colloquial or commonplace terms" and illustrations and begs his reader to consider two things as justification for this approach: "first, who I am, and second, who I am talking to."[25] This approach self-consciously adapts to the needs of a particular audience. The layout of the pages of *Peter Parley's Tales* reinforces a reading process directed at internalizing information. At the bottom of each page are a series of simple self-assessment questions testing whether the child reader has memorized the information on that page. For example, at the bottom of a page describing Naples are prompts, including, "What of the city Naples? Describe the country around it."[26] This catechistic style anticipates "Ithaca." Reading *Peter Parley's Tales* as an intertext for "Ithaca" suggests that this episode inscribes what is left when the historical narrative has been removed, leaving only questions and answers. In this case, "Ithaca" becomes a parodic performance of this model of childhood reading.

Portrait depicts the ways that Stephen's misinterpretation of himself according to ancient historical models makes him unable to discern the complexity of his modern experiences. When he approaches the rector's office, he thinks about the fact that the prefect of studies had forgotten his name. He then defends his name: "The great men in the history had names like that and nobody made fun of them" (*P* 48). That Stephen identifies the name "Dedalus" as a name from history, not myth, underscores for him the consequence of history books that blended them. Stephen endows his meeting with the rector with significance by connecting it to ancient and Catholic history. As he approaches the rector's office and sees portraits of "saints and great men of the order who were looking down on him silently as he passed" (*P* 48-9). He envisions in detail saint Ignatius Loyola "holding an open book and pointing to the words *Ad Majorem Dei Gloriam* in it" alongside portraits of several other Jesuits (*P* 49). However, the narrative frames these portraits with an admission that Stephen could not actually see them because it "was dark and silent and his eyes were weak and tired with tears so that he could not see" (*P* 48). Stephen's youth and his understanding of history lead him to misinterpret his conversation with the rector, which he thinks culminates in a victory that renders him "happy and free" (*P* 51). This naivete makes it all the more devastating when his father laughs about the same event by imitating the rector's description of the event: "*I told them all at dinner about it and Father Dolan and I and all of us we all had a hearty laugh together over it. Ha! Ha! Ha!*" (*P* 63). The narrative does not render Stephen's response to his father here, which suggests that his father's belittling re-telling of this story transforms him from an agent affirmed with historical significance into an object of derision without full awareness or control of the historical narratives in which he participates.

Translating Textual Rome

As *Portrait* suggests, Stephen's youth is marked by a struggle to escape from a historiographic imagination wedded to static, haunting images of great men, a struggle that is mobilized by an intuitive experience of language that grants him a new vantage point on ancient history. As Spoo notes, "[Stephen] is only gradually coming to realize that great men are participants in and products of a complex process involving both historical causation and historiographic production—the past and its textualization—from which these individuals emerge as freestanding, self-propelled agents only by courtesy of interpretive abstraction."[27] Joyce's reading of Guglielmo Ferrero's five-volume study, *The Greatness and Decline of Rome*, offered him an analytic historiographic alternative to his childhood reading. Ferrero defines his methodology as stemming from his "psychological and moral interest": "I have studied the history of Rome from the point of view of the transformation of manners, the increase of wants and luxury and of the standard of living and expenditure, from generation to generation."[28]

Ferrero's study of the age of Caesar describes the "historian's task" in a way that doubtless appealed to Joyce at a moment when he was beginning to conceptualize the rough outline of *Ulysses*:[29]

> Human history like all other phenomena of life and motion, is the unconscious product of an infinity of small and unnoticed efforts. Its work is done, spasmodically and in disorder, by single individuals or groups of

individuals, acting generally from immediate motives, with results which always transcend the knowledge and intentions of contemporaries, and are but seldom revealed, darkly and for a moment, to succeeding generations. To find a clue to the immediate, accidental, and transitory motives which have pricked on the men of the past to their labors; to describe vividly and whole-heartedly their vicissitudes and anxieties, their struggles and illusions, as they pursued their work; to discover how and why, through this work, the men of one generation have often, not satisfied with the passions which spurred them on to action, but effected some lasting transformation in the life of their society—this should be, in my opinion, the unfailing inspiration of the historian's task.[30]

The fact that *Ulysses*, in its own way, fulfills nearly all of the criteria Ferrero lays out here in his definition of historical work underscores the significance of Stephen's movement toward this kind of point of view in *Portrait* and *Ulysses*. The historiographic foundation of *Ulysses* depends vitally on the minute everyday actions, decisions, thoughts, and feelings of ordinary people who cannot know what the full consequences of their trivial and meaningful gestures alike might be. By following the development of Stephen's historical imagination from a childish worship of the great men of the past toward the kind of work Ferrero describes, we can better understand the process by which *Ulysses* becomes what Fritz Senn calls "History in a corrective sense," by which he means that the emphasis moves away "from the crucial exploits of great men and momentous changes to the humdrum, low-key texture of everyday events, whose weight is in their muted frequency . . ."[31]

This transformation can best be detected in *Portrait*'s verbal shifts, which demonstrate Stephen's maturation. Language and verbal play supply the critical support Stephen needs to alter his approach to history. At a key moment in *Portrait*, the "wayward rhythms" of language prompt him into a productive state of speculation. After Stephen experiences the ecstatic encounter with the bird-girl that seems to affirm his artistic future, he wanders aimlessly, unsure of the time, day, or week—realizing these make him aware that he has missed that day's lectures in English and French. Outside of the space of formalized knowledge and of an academic experience of language, Stephen's mind wanders among sounds:

The ivy whines upon the wall
And whines and twines upon the wall

The ivy whines upon the wall
The yellow ivy on the wall
Ivy, ivy up the wall.

Stephen initially rejects these verbal movements as "drivel," before an aesthetic experience of language quiets his inner censor. "Yellow ivy: that was all right," he thinks, "Yellow ivory also. And what about ivory ivy?" (*P* 156). His train of sonic associations leads him to a cognitive state where he can use language as an imaginative vehicle to open some distance from an oppressive and static sense of history:

> The word now shone in his brain, clearer and brighter than any ivory sawn from the mottled tusks of elephants. *Ivory, ivoire, avorio, ebur.* One of the first examples that he had learnt in Latin had run: *India mittit ebur;* and he recalled the shrewd northern face of the rector who had taught him to construe the Metamorphoses of Ovid in a courtly English, made whimsical by the mention of porkers and potsherds and chines of bacon. He had learnt what little he knew of the laws of Latin verse from a ragged book written by a Portuguese priest.
>
> *Contrahit orator, variant in carmine vates.*
>
> The crises and victories and secessions in Roman history were handed on to him in the trite words *in tanto discrimine* and he had tried to peer into the social life of the city of cities through the words *implere ollam denariorum* which the rector had rendered sonorously as the filling of a pot with denaries.
>
> (*P* 156)[32]

Stephen's repetition of "ivy" transmutes into "ivory," which opens into a process of translation that moves his thoughts across languages into Latin, where he can symbolically confront ivory as an image of empire expressed in the seemingly neutral Latin "India sends ivory," an expression that conceals the violence of imperial plunder. Stephen's thoughts suggest the rising significance of sociopolitical and material contexts for language that are inseparable from it. He thinks specifically of Father William Henry, his Latin teacher, and the distinctive British valences of his Latin instruction. He also envisions his Latin book as material—in this case, ragged—and as part of a national context (as it was written by the Portuguese Jesuit Emmanuel Alvarez). This moment shows a relatively new attention to the channels through which knowledge of the ancient world is transmitted. Stephen's memory of Ovid enables him to recognize the dissonance between his emerging perspective and Father Henry's defamiliarizing anglicization of Ovid. His movement away from a historical perspective interested in "the crises and victories and secessions in Roman history" and toward the material, economic conditions of unnamed Romans makes possible the historiography of *Ulysses* in its insistent writing of a microhistory of the lives of ordinary men and women on a single day.

Lessons in Forgetting

Over the course of his early career, Joyce used Roman and Greek history and culture to develop a useful rhetoric of apathy, which conceptually intersects with what Gregory Dobbins calls idleness. Idleness, he argues, distinguishes the ideology and aesthetic of Revivalism in its promotion of various kinds of productivity and labor on behalf of Ireland and the more experimental modernist aesthetic associated with Wilde, Joyce, O'Brien, and Beckett.[33] *Ulysses*, Dobbins notes, "negates those dominant values, motifs, and forms associated with the Revival in order to clear a conceptual space for something else. For this act of unworking to occur, the very role of the intellectual charged with the production of a national culture must be interrogated and dismantled."[34] Irish idleness, Dobbins argues, is not true in actuality but rather is "functionally important in a rhetorical and political sense."[35] Joyce's post-1904 creative process shows his struggle for a form that is grounded in detachment, active passivity, and at least partial forgetting. Stephen's memory in *Ulysses* poses an existential and psychological challenge that the novel's style, in its commitment to perpetual reinvention, seeks to overcome. This ongoing process is visible in Joyce's fiction and in the paratexts that surround his work; it comes to fruition in the radical play of *Finnegans Wake*, which, as Spoo notes, takes "forgetting as the first condition of aesthetic activity."[36] Ancient history offers Stephen a pathway toward forgetting until it, too, becomes part of the history he tries to forget.

One of the best-remembered lines of *Ulysses* is Stephen's to Mr. Deasy: "History ... is a nightmare from which I am trying to awake" (*U* 2.377). Moments earlier, Stephen himself reflected on such tag lines in his history lesson: "That phrase the world had remembered. A dull ease of the mind"

(*U* 2.15). The problem with the phrases the world had remembered, Stephen realizes, is that they suffice as generalized knowledge that overlooks the complex processes and lost potentialities of history. In the case of his specific lesson on Pyrrhus, the phrase the world remembered formed as a substitute for the violence of war and for the alternate outcomes ousted by the historical event. "Nestor" dramatizes the process by which Stephen is trying to "awake" and demonstrates the novel's sense of what such an awakening must entail. Even though *Ulysses* is structured in a decidedly non-teleological way, taking place on an ordinary single day, he makes progress in his confrontation with history that is made possible by his engagement with ancient history in the lesson he teaches.

Stephen's history lesson begins with him asking a student to reproduce details about Pyrrhus's war against the Romans on behalf of Tarentum. In his lesson, Stephen echoes the catechistic structure of *Peter Parley's Tales* by moving from the specific question "what city sent for him" to the more rhetorically diffuse "well?" until the boy's knowledge fails him when he forgets the place, but remembers the date of the Battle of Asculum, which Stephen himself reads from a "gorescarred" book.[37] When the boy forgets the location of the battle, Stephen undermines the notion of epic history as "fabled by the daughters of memory" by thinking, "and yet it was in some way if not as memory fabled it" (*U* 2.7–8). The awkwardness of this construction dissipates the agency of memory in an episode that is dedicated, in part, to scrutinizing the cultural, social, and psychological damage wrought by various kinds of memory.

As Joyce well knew while writing during a period of global and national violence, the potential damage of historical memory was immediate and urgent. The Battle of Asculum offers Joyce a useful anachronism, a historically distant way of responding to war, violence, and a costly victory, issues that will eventually determine the futures of many of Stephen's students. As James Fairhall notes, the images of ancient battle in "Nestor" evoke images of the First World War, the Rising, and the Irish Civil War for an Irish readership—these events loom over the classroom and will, in all likelihood, claim the lives of at least some of Stephen's students. Through Stephen's history lesson, *Ulysses* begins, as Luke Gibbons argues, to lay the "groundwork for an entire generation coming to terms with the often unacknowledged psychological abrasions of the war of independence and the Civil War."[38] In the absence of geographical knowledge, Cochrane repeats what everyone remembers, "Another victory like that and we are done for," which prompts Stephen to reflect on the living force of the "phrase the world had remembered." This moment of recitation leads to a series of battle images of a "corpsestrewn plain" where a general speaks to his officers (*U* 2.14, 16). Stephen then generalizes this conflict, "Any general to any officers. They lend ear" (*U* 2.17). The Pyrrhic victory hangs in the classroom as an unrealized reflection of Ireland's subterranean commitment to an ideology of failure, a dimension of Irish identity that Joyce scrutinized throughout his writings. As Robert Kee notes, the Irish valorization of martyrs such as Robert Emmet emerges from the "very need to ennoble failure. For tragic failure was to become part of Ireland's identity, something indistinguishable from 'the cause' itself."[39] "Nestor" suggests that this task requires Stephen and his students to find a way to forget the past, even momentarily, so that a different kind of story and history might begin to take shape. The history lesson establishes human perception, knowledge, and history as arenas of conflict between a "dull ease of the mind" and a historical nightmare. Both options anticipate Stephen's discovery that his mind is where he "must kill the priest and the king" (*U* 15.4437–8). Stephen's students help him find what he actually needs in that moment, a partial amnesia that will loosen the past's grasp on him.

Forgetting historical facts opens a space for verbal play to emerge as an imaginative escape mechanism. When Armstrong answers the question "Do you know anything about Pyrrhus?" with "Pyrrhus, a pier," Stephen gladly follows him out of historical recitation into a ludic flight from the past with the ultimately failed joke, "Kingstown pier ... Yes, a disappointed bridge" (*U* 2.21, 2.26). The sonic association between "Pyrrhus" and "pier" initiates a movement out of Asculum and into the space of Dublin, a movement Stephen quickly realizes reproduces his sense of entrapment when he thinks of Haines and concludes, "For them too history was a tale like any other too often heard, their land a pawnshop" (*U* 2.46–7). Stephen displays his imaginative agility when he takes a new approach to ancient history grounded in the Aristotelian concept of potentiality (in the *Metaphysics*). Aristotle's theory of the form of forms enables Stephen to develop the line of thinking he began as a boy in *Portrait* when he wondered if a green rose might exist. Here, he articulates this problem historically: "Had Pyrrhus not fallen by a beldam's hand in Argos or Julius

Caesar not been knifed to death" (*U* 2.48–49). This moment asserts the revitalizing power of the imagination against the contingency of historical experience. Rather than serving as figures to be memorized, Pyrrhus and Caesar become bearers of possibility, collaborating in Stephen's attempt to imagine a different world and identity. As Gifford points out, the claim in Aristotle's *Poetics* that "the distinction between historian and poet . . . consists really in that the one describes the thing that has been, and the other a kind of thing that might be" (*UA* 31). As Margaret McBride puts it, Stephen's appropriation of Aristotle's concept of the "form of forms" is especially important because Stephen applies it to the artist and "the poet's goal is not merely to know or understand the factual, external universe: it is to *create* a fictive universe."[40] This fictive universe grants its participants a sense of potential that might be useful in the world. Stephen's imaginative turn to Aristotle enables him, however temporarily, to assert the power of literature against history as a means for changing the educational process of indoctrinating students to a cultural system that worships death and failure. This movement captures in miniature a crucial aspect of the historical work of *Ulysses*, which rewrites both myth and history to offer a modern model of the heroic grounded in small-scale successes and, ultimately, survival.

Once it is clear that there will be no return to the history lesson, Stephen's students signal their early participation in a culture immersed in death through their demand that he tell them a ghost story. Rather than telling the boys a ghost story, Stephen opens Milton's *Lycidas*, a pastoral elegy written for Milton's friend, Edward King, who drowned. That Stephen labels *Lycidas* a ghost story undermines the drive of the poem, to envision the immortal resurrected life of Edward King through the poet's imagination. Stephen thus implicitly transforms the mode of revival from resurrection of an eternal memory into the creation of a ghost, or, as Stephen later says in the National Library, "one who has faded into impalpability through death, through absence, through change of manners" (*U* 9.147–9).

The process of what happens in the classroom during and after the encounter with *Lycidas* exposes Stephen's distance from Revivalism as an ideology. Stephen asks the students where they begin in the poem, to which Comyn replies, "Weep no more," which is the opening of the penultimate stanza. When a student asks Stephen to give the story of the poem first, Stephen demurs and replies "After," which further amplifies his revision of Milton's narrative through his fragmented, non-contextual mode of presenting it in the classroom (*U* 2.57). He then commands Talbot to recite the poem and he "recited jerks of verse with odd glances at the text" (*U* 2. 62–3). This mode of recitation suggests that the poem does not find its way easily into the mouths and minds of his students. In place of the story, students confront an image of poetic resurrection recast as a ghost story in a set of images that distantly evoke Stephen's own haunted memories of his mother: "*Weep no more, woful shepherds, weep no more / For Lycidas, your sorrow, is not dead, / Sunk though he be beneath the watery floor*" (*U* 2.64–6). In this recitation, versions of Stephen's personal, literary, political past come back as a force that he must contend with as he performs a role that will help shape the historical imaginations of his students.

Stephen's memory, as Cheng observes, is one of the central problems of *Ulysses*, and the history lesson serves as a moment of collective forgetting that reinforces the notion that he "sees too much and cannot forget."[41] We see how easily the past haunts him in "Telemachus"—the appearance of the sea coupled with Buck calling it "our mighty mother" leads Stephen to envision the traumatizing details of her death and her ghost. The appearance of a cloud prompts the thought sequence that leads him to confront his mother as the "Ghoul! Chewer of corpses!" (*U* 1.85). By contrast, the same cloud momentarily evokes existential dread realized as an encounter with an image of deep history as "a dead sea in a dead land, grey and old" in Bloom, but he is able to recover from that experience by returning to the feeling of his own body: "Well, I am here now. Yes, I am here now. Morning mouth bad images. Got up wrong side of the bed" (*U* 4.232–4). Likewise, in "Sirens," Bloom escapes from the homosocial ritual of bonding over deeply felt grief for national martyrs by returning imaginatively to his own experience, which protects him from the collective impulse to "wipe away a tear for martyrs that want to, dying to, die" (*U* 11.1101–2). When Ben Dollard sings "The Croppy Boy," Bloom translates the words to his own experience: "I too. Last of my race. Milly young student. Well, my fault perhaps. No son. Rudy. Too late now. Or if not? If not? If still?" (*U* 11.1066–7). Bloom's movement away from a grief-stricken national memory to his own private memories restores him to an Aristotelian state of potentiality as he considers his own life. Likewise, his turn away from the existential horror evoked by confronting the deep past to his own body allows him to consider returning to Sandow's exercises in order to make his body stronger (*U* 4.234). The movements of Bloom's mind reveal his genuine engagement with himself and the world in terms of dynamic potentiality. History is not a nightmare for Bloom because it is continually in flux and is open to his inner reshaping of it, moment by moment. Though Stephen theorizes it, Bloom actually experiences the "actuality of the possible as possible" (*U* 2.67). This inner dimension of Bloom's mind comes to the foreground in "Circe," when we see harbored in his psyche a fantasy of Ireland as a "new Bloomusalem in the Nova Hibernia of the future." In this fantasy, he is what "an old resident" recognizes as "a credit to [his] country" and what "an applewoman" concludes is a "man like Ireland wants" (*U* 15.1537–46). This fantasy resonates with Joyce's own vision of Ireland's past in terms of cultural hybridity against the kinds of xenophobia in *Ulysses* that would deny Bloom's Irishness.

The structure of what might be taken as his failed history lesson—which moves from forgetting into verbal play into a partial, fragmented, halting recitation of *Lycidas* as a ghost story—enables Stephen momentarily to experience the past in a way that resembles Bloom's experience. Stephen's mental return to Aristotle during the recitation of *Lycidas* leads him not to Pyrrhus and Caesar as great men destroyed by chance or treachery but rather to his own recent history. This moment thus signifies a movement away from familiar structures of knowledge, which interpreted his experiences according to the narratives of great men. He recalls sitting in the library of Saint Genevieve in Paris reading Aristotle. His process of remembering his own past—rather than engaging in the collective act of taking in Milton's words—generates a remarkable personal metaphor for Stephen's mind: "Fed and feeding brains about me: under glowlamps, impaled, with faintly beating feelers: and in my mind's darkness a sloth of the underworld, reluctant, shy of brightness, shifting her dragon scaly folds. Thought is the thought of thought. Tranquil brightness ..." (*U* 2.71–4). Dobbins reads this moment as a signal of Stephen's state of impotentiality and of the subversive idleness (here registered as sloth) at the center of his imagination, an idleness that will protect him from the sacrifices of labor that Ireland, church, and family might demand he make.[42] This underworld creature also signals Stephen's creation of an artistic metaphor for himself that conceptually extends the bird-girl and Dedalus in *Portrait* as external avatars of his creativity with a crucial difference: this metaphor is internalized within his mind rather than projected into the world. Stephen here generates a vision of himself as harboring a figure of pure imagination, the "geen wothe" of his childhood musings that has become "an actuality of the possible as possible."

Stephen is pulled out of his reflections when Talbot's memory fails him and he repeats the line "Through the dear might of Him that walked the waves," having apparently forgotten what follows. This moment of forgetting ironically undermines the poem itself as a tribute to the memory of Edward King. When Talbot slides his book into his satchel because it is time for hockey, Stephen asks, "Have I heard all?" a question that suggests his own lack of intimate familiarity with either the end of the poem, the routine of the class in its recitation of the poem, or both. This moment of collective forgetting and abandonment of the poem undercuts the full force of the poem's final resurrection imagery. Rather than drawing on the poem as a model for poetic revival, Stephen and his students half-remember it from a position of apathy, which is, as it turns out, precisely what Stephen needs.

After the history lesson has concluded, with the students telling him that it is a half day and time for hockey, Stephen gives them a riddle. The timing of this suggests that the riddle emerges both as a culmination of and an alternative to the history lesson. Stephen presents the riddle:

> *The cock crew,*
> *The sky was blue:*
> *The bells in heaven*
> *Were striking eleven.*
> *'Tis time for this poor soul*
> *To go to heaven.*
>
> (*U* 2.102–7)

Of course, none of Stephen's students can produce the answer to this riddle—"The fox burying his grandmother under a hollybush"—because this is not actually an answer in any sense that is familiar to Stephen's students (*U* 2.115). Stephen subverts the structure of the pedagogical exchange by offering his students the riddle and another riddle as the answer, without spelling out the possible logical connection between the two. By opening a stubborn gap between question and answer, Stephen's classical pedagogy suggests that the purpose of the classical history lesson is not to demonstrate knowledge as obedience but rather to manage ambiguity. This structure unravels the persistent historiographic structure writ large in Joyce's depiction of classical historical pedagogy. Unlike *Peter Parley's Tales* and Stephen's own reproduction of the catechistic mode moments earlier, the riddle disrupts a process that requires students to internalize historical data and unconsciously incorporate it into their emerging identities. By changing what happens between question and answer, the riddle leaves students in a state of potentially liberating openness and perplexity, a cognitive state the rest of *Ulysses* depends on.

Siren Songs and Mistaken Histories

Stephen's most successful adoption of an apathetic, detached historical viewpoint occurs in "Eumaeus." Once again, Joyce turns to the ancient world to work out the terms of this historical detachment—which, far from being ahistorical, is rather an emotionally distant view of history as open to analysis and change, a view that offers an enabling alternative to history as nightmare. In this context, it makes sense that Stephen tells Bloom to take away the knife because it "reminds [him] of Roman history" (*U* 16.816). This request reproduces the turns away from Roman history running through Joyce's fiction, most recently in "Aeolus," in which Professor MacHugh dismisses Roman civilization as "vast ... but vile" (*U* 7.489). Stephen's desire not to be reminded of a history marked by the ennobled violence of great men reinforces the position of controlled forgetting that he discovered in "Nestor." From a position of willed disavowal of Roman historical memory, he is able to distance himself from Irish history and tells Bloom, "We can't change the country. Let us change the subject" (*U* 16.1171). In "Eumaeus," Stephen has decided, as Joyce did, to "let the ruins rot," and in so doing to change the subject, in multiple senses. Over the course of the day, Stephen has learned to identify history as a Siren song without being destroyed by it.

The end of "Eumaeus" suggests that Joyce used Homer's *Odyssey*—and, more particularly, the Sirens—in order to articulate the historiographic vision Stephen has acquired. To understand why the Sirens might have been useful in this project required a brief return to that Homeric story. In the 12th book of the *Odyssey*, Odysseus sails past the Sirens. His crew's ears stopped with wax, he is tied to the mast, reveling in the ecstatic torment of the beautiful song he hears. As Circe warns Odysseus, the Sirens, sitting in a meadow littered with the bones of their victims, ensnare men with their sweet voices and foreclose their homecoming. Odysseus never sees the mass grave Circe describes, and he discovers that the most seductive power of the Sirens' song rests not only in the beauty of the Sirens' voices but also in their promise of an experience of comprehensive knowledge:

> Odysseus! Come here! You are well-known
> from many stories! Glory of the Greeks!
> Now stop your ship and listen to our voices.
> All those who pass this way hear honeyed song,
> poured from our mouths. The music brings them joy,
> and they go on their way with greater knowledge,
> since we know everything the Greeks and Trojans
> suffered in Troy, by gods' will; and we know
> whatever happens anywhere on earth.

> (*O* 12.183–91)

The allure of Odysseus' past threatens his future as the Sirens tempt him to suspend his life listening to songs extolling his Trojan history.[43] The Sirens claim a totalizing, all-encompassing knowledge of the past and present—they can, as Andrew Ford suggests, 'offer the entire *Iliad* and more'[44]—and they lure Odysseus with the promise of endowing him with this kind of full knowledge. By dramatizing this experience of poetry and of history as potentially fatal, this scene suggests that Homer understood the tantalizing danger of such promises.[45] And nearly three millennia later, so too did Joyce, whose fiction depicts Stephen's attempt to manage the Siren song of history without being destroyed by it. Odysseus's decision not to stop his ears with wax offers an apt metaphor for the state toward which Stephen strives in *Ulysses* as he searches for a vantage point from which he can experience history in a productive way without turning away from it. Odysseus survives the Siren song because he remains still—he is tied to the mast of his own free will and cannot be moved or consumed by the song.

Joyce's deployment of the Sirens in "Eumaeus" hints at the significance of Stephen's movement toward useful apathy on June 16, 1904. At the end of

"Eumaeus," as Stephen and Bloom walk to 7 Eccles Street, Stephen lectures Bloom on music. His thoughts turn to "an old German song of Johannes Jeep about the clear sea and the voices of Sirens, sweet murderers of men" (*U* 16.1812–13). Gifford translates the entire passage from which Stephen sings as:

> From the Sirens' craftiness
> Poets make poems
> That they with their loveliness
> Have drawn many men into the sea
> For their song resounds so sweetly,
> That the sailors fall asleep,
> The ship is brought into misfortune,
> And all becomes evil.

At the end of the episode, Stephen sings "more boldly, but not loudly" his mangled version of the final lines, including the invented German line, "*Und alle Schiffe brücken*" (and all the ships are broken) (*U* 16.1884). "Boggled . . . a bit," Bloom listens to Stephen sing but remains distant from his "phenomenally beautiful tenor voice" by his own inner musings on Stephen's possible future as a singer (*U* 16.1814, 1820). Bloom resists the seduction of the past, in part because it seems likely that he is not actually listening to the words Stephen sings and translates for him. The novel's final Siren song offers a telling glimpse at its perspective on the Sirens' promise of totalizing historical knowledge and the "craftiness" from which "poets make poems." Through its mistakes and its performative context, Stephen sings a new kind of Siren song, one grounded in error as a "portal of discovery" and a productive kind of faltering knowledge.

The end of "Eumaeus" illustrates the novel's commitment to faltering knowledge by moving the narrative focalization to the driver who watches, but cannot fully hear, Stephen and Bloom:

> The driver never said a word, good, bad or indifferent, but merely watched the two figures, *as he sat on his lowbacked car*, both black, one full, one lean, walk towards the railway bridge, *to be married by Father Maher*. As they walked they at times stopped and walked again continuing their *tete a tete* (which of course he was utterly out of) about sirens, enemies of man's reason, mingled with a number of other topics of the same category, usurpers, historical cases of the kind while the man in the sweeper car or you might as well call it the sleeper car who in any case couldn't possibly hear because

they were too far simply sat in his seat near the end of lower Gardiner street *and looked after their lowbacked car.*

(*U* 16.1885–94)

The ending of "Eumaeus" denies the epistemological seduction of the Siren song. Even if a reader is unaware of Stephen's German mistake, she is immersed in an explicitly limited narrative point of view that "merely" watches the novel's two primary male characters walk away without hearing more than stray phrases that collectively hint at a miniaturized version of *Ulysses* itself from usurpers up until this moment. In the *Odyssey*, the Sirens promise to tell Odysseus something like the *Iliad*, but their song is explicitly excluded from Homer's epic in a way that reinforces a gap between what the Sirens know and what Homer's audience can know. In a way that inverts the Sirens' promise to deliver full knowledge, "Eumaeus" ends by disclosing to its readers that which they do not and will never know. Increasingly distant from the scene, the driver occupies a position of readerly partial knowledge that can never be overcome.

Early on in Stephen's history lesson, as already noted, his student recalls the tag line of the Pyrrhic victory, which prompts Stephen to reflect upon the "dull ease of the mind" in its perception of history. The narrative voice at the end of "Eumaeus" performs such cognitive dullness through the italicized verses (as Gifford notes, from "The Lowbacked Car") that intrude upon the narration. The narrative placement of the driver in his "lowbacked car" almost compulsively prompts the narrative voice to continue the poem, which inadvertently suggests Stephen and Bloom will be married by Father Maher. That which the narrative voice already knows, in this case, the echo of a previous poem, blocks the full perception of the present moment. In a way that shows the human historical imagination at work, "Eumaeus" ends with the past confronting the present in such a way that reinforces the impossibility of full knowledge of either.

In his study of the modernist *Bildungsroman*, Gregory Castle notes the problem that knowledge poses to the development of Stephen Dedalus who, at the end of *Portrait*, is able to "discern a pattern of violence connected with the acquisition of knowledge and to assert himself successfully against it and, to some degree, his own desire, only to find himself still under its sway."[46] Joyce's depiction of ancient history over the span of his early fiction shows him grappling with the ancient world as that which might be known and as that which Stephen hopes to disavow.

Stephen began June 16 in a state of despair, as he was haunted by the ghost of his mother. At the outset of his history lesson in "Nestor," his inner state is reflected when he recalls the words of William Blake and imagines that he hears "the ruin of all space, shattered glass and toppling masonry, and time one livid final flame" (*U* 2.8–9). For Stephen, history is what Stephen Kern calls a "panorama of disaster" marked by unceasing violence.[47] Confronting his personal and political past threatens to destroy him, leaving him strewn among the ruins of a violent history. Stephen's struggle underscores Joyce's imaginative achievement in Rome, where adopting an apathetic pose toward Roman history by deciding to let its ruins rot formed a necessary prelude to his most innovative literary period. The end of "Eumaeus" reshapes the ancient mythological figure of the Sirens to suggest that Stephen and Joyce may not awake from history as a nightmare, but over the wanderings of an ordinary day, the possibility remains that they might discover a portal made possible by their own mistakes, disavowals, and failures of memory.

3

Joyce, Homer, and the Seductions of Reading

In the ninth episode of *Ulysses*, Stephen Dedalus articulates a theory of composition and reception to a group of skeptical listeners in the National Library. In his theory, he insists on the significance of the lived experience of the author to the creation of literary works, and he demands a contextual mode of reading that keeps the author in view. During a brief pause, he recalls his thoughts in "Nestor" and "ponders things that were not: what Caesar would have lived to do had he believed the soothsayer: what might have been: possibilities of the possible as possible: things not known" (*U* 9.348–50). Stephen's mode of Shakespearean reception leads him into a thought process that engages with possibility alongside actuality in a way that enables personal transformation. At the end of *Portrait*, he saw his future as an Icarian enterprise to "forge in the smithy of [his] soul the uncreated conscience of [his] race." In *Ulysses*, he finds himself back in Ireland, unacknowledged and aimless. Perhaps more than anything, he craves change and envisions literature as enacting radical personal, psychological, social, and political transformation. In the Library, he confronts the failures of the literary tradition to transform readers. He looks at the books around him and thinks, "Coffined thoughts around me, in mummycases, embalmed in spice of words . . . They are still. Once quick in the brains of men" (*U* 9.352–3, 9.356).

The demands *Ulysses* makes on its readers emerge in part from the novel's struggle against a future in which it too might become a set of "coffined thoughts . . . embalmed in spice of words." The unfolding series of stylistic innovations initiated midway through *Ulysses* signifies one strategy by which the novel forces its readers into imaginative agility. Stephen serves as an example of such agility on Sandymount Strand when he composes his poem, itself a work that emerges from a tension between dynamism and stasis, realized as the life-giving movement of the "womb" and its deadening rhyming double, the "tomb" (*U* 3.402). The novel's self-conscious depictions of creativity and reception suggest a defense of the transformative power of the literary tradition and the process of reading. Most of the novel's depictions of reading processes focus on failure that stems largely from psychological, cognitive, or ideological rigidity. Its representations of static art and entrenched modes of reading highlight the imaginative and actual damage wrought by various forms of intransigence.

In this chapter, I turn to Joyce's self-conscious anticipation, interrogation, and rewriting of the reception of his fiction in dialogue with his contemporary society and with the classical literary tradition. My analysis will begin with perhaps the most well-covered issue in Joyce studies, Joyce's reading of the *Odyssey*. However, rather than returning to a methodology that considers how the *Odyssey* might help us to understand *Ulysses*, I pursue a question articulated by Fritz Senn, who asks "how the two epics electrify each other."[1] More specifically, I am interested in how two of the most self-reflexive works in the Western tradition illuminate each other in terms of their shared interest in reading as an individual and social act. Read in tandem, the *Odyssey* and *Ulysses* illustrate the dangers and seductions of stories and the illusory nature of aesthetic detachment. In different ways, each work promotes an ethical mode of reading grounded in empathetic involvement and co-authorship that keeps in view the seductions and perils of the act of interpretation.

Joyce's way of reading the classical tradition in terms of its dynamic potential depended vitally on his reading of classical women. Helen and Penelope, Joyce's work emphasizes, might be taken as static embodiments of female transgression and virtue respectively. The genetic materials of *Ulysses* suggest that Joyce's reading of women in the classical tradition exposes the violent scapegoating of women that arises from static readings. From its beginnings, *Ulysses* strives to envision a fully dynamic modern female character as an alternative. His reading notes suggest his engagement with classical women as potentially revealing figures who lay bare latent sources of social and psychological stasis. Mythic female figures played an essential role in his process of writing his way toward perhaps his major innovation in the epic tradition, the ecstatic conclusion of Molly Bloom, a modern Penelope who has the last word.

Buck Mulligan Thinks of Homer

"Scylla and Charybdis" is, as John Nash notes, a "key document" in Joyce's "representation of reception."[2] It is also a key document that makes visible his reading of Homer at two significant moments in his composition of *Ulysses*. By all accounts, even though "Scylla and Charybdis" is the novel's ninth episode, it was one of the first parts of the novel Joyce drafted. In 1912, he delivered a series of lectures on *Hamlet* at the Universita del Popolo that formed the core of Stephen's Shakespeare theory (*JJ* 345).[3] In January 1917, he wrote to Ezra Pound that the only episode he had completed and could send on was "Scylla and Charybdis." If "Scylla and Charybdis" seemed to have served as a kind of conceptual anchor in the development of *Ulysses*, it also served as a turning point in his unfolding understanding of his novel. At the end of 1918, he wrote "New Year's Eve, 1918| End of First Part of Ulysses" on the last page of the faircopy version of "Scylla and Charybdis" as if, Michael Groden notes, "to indicate that one phase of *Ulysses* was ending and something new was about to begin."[4]

"Scylla and Charybdis" shows Joyce's pivot from a novel that was mostly stylistically stable and concerned with the inner lives of Stephen and Bloom toward a novel defined not by its characters' experiences but by a series of bold stylistic experiments. It is a textual site of intense intersection between the classical and experimental elements of Joyce's writing and as such, it offers a unique archive to understand how these elements enhanced one another as Joyce made critical decisions about his novel and about its relationship to the Homeric tradition. "Scylla and Charybdis" also makes visible the deep preoccupation with interpretation that runs through both the *Odyssey* and *Ulysses*, creating the foundation of self-consciousness that is so important to each work. That Joyce adapts classical literature to create a uniquely self-conscious art is self-evident—naming a character "Stephen Dedalus" and a novel "Ulysses" would be all the evidence one would need to make this case. However, "Scylla and Charybdis" suggests that the classical tradition as he read it not only accommodated but also shared his self-conscious attention to composition and reception.

Joyce's use of Homer generated a rich critical conversation that started before the first publication of *Ulysses*.[5] My own work has benefited from this vibrant critical conversation as I have sought to ask how *Ulysses* and the *Odyssey* teach us to read one another and, more generally, how to read. Germane to my discussion of Joyce and Homer is the following contextual information. Joyce became interested in Homer at a young age when he read Charles Lamb's *The Adventures of Ulysses* and admired its hero's cunning and perseverance. Records indicate that he was interested in writing a short story about the wanderings of a modern Ulysses through Dublin for *Dubliners* and later scrapped that plan. As Hugh Kenner argues, there was no singular, static Homer on which Joyce relied in his conceptualization of *Ulysses*; as I have argued elsewhere, this multiplicity is essential to understanding the extraordinary versatility of Homer for Joyce's modernist project.[6] When W.B. Stanford asked Stanislaus Joyce which books on Homer Joyce used, the list he supplied illustrates the range of Joyce's interests: "Virgil, Ovid, Dante, Racine, Fénelon, Phillips, Tennyson, d'Annunzio, Hauptmann, as well as Samuel Butler's *The Authoress of the Odyssey* and Victor Bérard's *Les Phéniciens et l'Odyssée* and the translations by Butler and Cowper."[7] This list offers a glimpse at Joyce's wide-ranging reading process across genres, epochs, and languages that complicates the persistent notion, active since Joyce circulated schemas hinting at his novel's underlying structural design, that the *Odyssey* was primarily a source of mythic order for *Ulysses*. When we read Joyce reading Homer, we recognize how much reading Homer facilitated Joyce's own urgent reflections on the nature of reading as an individual, social, and always historical act. And, conversely, Joyce's construction and interrogation of audiences and their reading processes in *Ulysses* offers us a new lens for appreciating the *Odyssey*'s construction of bardic performances and their audiences, a topic that has long interested classics scholars but has remained in the background in Joyce studies.[8]

Although its title points readers toward Homer's *Odyssey* and the tradition it created, *Ulysses* contains only two named references to Homer, both in "Scylla and Charybdis." One was added late in Joyce's composition process to the scene near the end of the episode when Buck is chastising Stephen for his antagonism toward the Irish Literary Revival. Specifically, he is chiding Stephen for his negative review of Lady Gregory's "Poets and Dreamers" in *Longworth's Daily Express*. In 1903, Joyce criticized Lady Gregory for championing a land "almost fabulous in its sorrow and senility," which, Gifford concludes, articulates Joyce's position that "the senile dreams of the past were hardly sufficient to a vital national literature" (*UA* 254). Buck asks Stephen, "couldn't you do the Yeats touch?" (*U* 9.1160–1). He then paraphrases Yeats's preface to Lady

Gregory's 1902 *Cuchulain of Muirthemne: The Story of the Men of the Red Branch of Ulster* (*UA* 254) by saying, "The most beautiful book that has come out of our country in my time. One thinks of Homer" (*U* 9.1165–6). The genetic record shows that Joyce added to the end of Buck's statement the phrase "one thinks of Homer" at a relatively late stage of revision, after the episode was published in *The Little Review*, after he sent the *Ulysses* schema to Carlo Linati in September 1920, and after he himself had dedicated more years to thinking of Homer as he worked on his novel. This genetic background helps us to recognize the ways this episode is self-consciously asking, what does it mean for "one"—some non-specified person—to "[think] of Homer"?

"Scylla and Charybdis" takes great care to deconstruct the notion shared by most of the men in the library of a universal reader, "one" who might think of Homer. For example, in the opening sentences of the episode, Thomas Lyster, who is mainly referred to as "the quaker librarian" rather than by name, uses the following phrases to elaborate his reading of Hamlet via Goethe": "as one sees in real life" and "One always feels that Goethe's judgments are so true" (*U* 9.4–11). The others echo this universalized, depersonalized model of reading. When Stephen reminds the men that Aristotle was once Plato's student, John Eglinton replies, "And has remained so, one should hope . . . One can see him, a model schoolboy with his diploma under his arm" (*U* 9.58–9). Earlier in the novel, Stephen recalls his former literary ambitions to have his epiphanies sent to all of the libraries of the world for "Someone [who] was to read them there after a few thousand years . . . When one reads these strange pages of one long gone one feels that one is at one with one who once . . . (*U* 3.143–6; ellipses in the original). As he expounds his Shakespeare theory in the library, Stephen makes clear that he has outgrown the fantasy of an impersonal reader. For Stephen, and for Joyce, to think of Homer is to think about the specific conditions of reading both historically and socially.

Joyce's Phaeacians and the seductions of aesthetic distance

From its first lines, "Scylla and Charybdis" demonstrates a conflict between Stephen's high-stakes investment in literature and the detached model of reading shared by most of the men in the library that is grounded in ease and reassurance. The episode opens with, "Urbane, to comfort them, the quaker librarian purred" (*U* 9.1). This phrase establishes an important value shared by the men in the library, that speech and language in their most cultivated, sophisticated form are meant as sources of comfort. The librarian's comforting reading of *Hamlet* displays his readerly habits, habits the episode ultimately challenges: "And we have, have we not, those priceless pages of *Wilhelm Meister*. A great poet on a great brother poet. A hesitating soul taking arms against a sea of troubles, torn by conflicting doubts, as one sees in real life" (*U* 9.2–4). This statement begins by establishing a collective readership that is bound together by an empty rhetorical affirmation ("have we not"). It proceeds by abstraction— not naming any of the poets, characters, or readers—thus setting up the episode's conflict between Platonic and Aristotelian philosophy. Although this statement attests to concern for the analogical connection between literature and "real life," it undercuts such connection by referring vaguely to "one" who makes the connection and by suggesting that, in fact, the literary tradition may actually be a hermetically sealed conversation among men as brother poets.

The conversation that follows develops the men's desire to view both literature and life from a position of detachment. George Russell, for example, does not want to know about "how [Shakespeare] lived" and suggests, "as for living our servants can do that for us" (*U* 9.185–6). He concludes, "We have *King Lear*: and it is immortal" and the narrative suggests he speaks the collective opinion of the group by noting that, "Mr Best's face, appealed to, agreed" (*U* 9.188–9). Moments later, Russell links Revivalist aesthetics with his admiration for Homer's Phaeacians:

> People do not know how dangerous lovesongs can be, the auric egg of Russell warned occultly. The movements which work revolutions in the world are born out of the dreams and visions in a peasant's heart on the hillside. For them the earth is not an exploitable ground but the living mother. The rarefied air of the academy and the arena produce the sixshilling novel, the musichall song. France produces the finest flower of corruption in Mallarmé but the desirable life is revealed only to the poor of heart, the life of Homer's Phaeacians.
>
> (*U* 9.103–10)

Russell here recycles tropes and clichés of the Revival, including the "dreams and visions in a peasant's heart on the hillside," the sense of the earth as "the living mother," and his rejection of both the academy and popular culture. The reference to the Homeric Phaeacians appeared from the first extant draft of "Scylla and Charybdis" onward, which means that until Joyce's late stages of revision, this reference was the only named reference to Homer in *Ulysses*. Russell's Phaeacians affirm the value of the rural fantasies of the Revival.

Joyce's Homeric research offers possible insight into how he might have apprehended the Phaeacians. As is well known, Victor Bérard's *Les Phéniciens et L'Odyssée* sparked Joyce's imagination about the possibility that the *Odyssey* had Semitic origins, which affirmed the decision he had already made to create a Jewish Odysseus in Leopold Bloom. As Michael Seidel has shown, Joyce took from Bérard the notion that the epic narrative could serve as a map of sorts, and he mapped the trajectories of Odysseus's travels as presented by Bérard onto the movements of his characters in Dublin.[9] As Hugh Kenner argues, Joyce's attraction to Bérard can be at least partly explained by his commitment to a notion of the realist texture of the Homeric epics, which could be associated with actual places that might be excavated by a modern-day archaeologist such as Heinrich Schliemann or Wilhelm Dörpfeld.[10] Joyce's notebooks show that he was also an attentive reader of Bérard, whose arguments depended on the kind of etymological play for which Joyce was also known. For example, as Seidel recounts, Joyce transcribed several of Bérard's etymologies in his notebooks, including the etymology of "Charybdis" as "Hole of Loss."[11]

In his notebooks, Joyce annotates several of Bérard's claims about the Phaeacians and about their island, Scheria. One entry reads "Alkinoos speech interpolater."[12] In the section Joyce annotates, Bérard is analyzing the exchange between the Phaeacian King, Alcinous, and Odysseus at the end of Demodocus's performance.[13] Alcinous asks Odysseus why he weeps and who he is, and this exchange leads Odysseus to recount his adventures. Bérard argues that Alcinous's speech at the end of Book 8 can be divided into two parts, one of which is an interpolation that should be ignored. The first part, Bérard writes, is "*parfaitement utile et raisonnable*" (perfectly useful and reasonable)—in the lines to which he refers, Alcinous is noticing Odysseus's tears in response to Demodocus's song, explaining his rationale for ending the performance, and asking him who he is.[14] Then, Bérard notes, Alcinous shifts into "*maladroite niaiserie*" (clumsy nonsense) when he starts to talk of the magical Phaeacian ships in lines translated by Samuel Butcher and Andrew Lang as: "For the Phaeacians have no pilots nor any rudders after the manner of other ships, but their barques themselves understand the thoughts and intents of men; they know the cities and fat fields of every people, and most swiftly they traverse the gulf of the salt sea, shrouded in mist and in cloud, and never do they go in fear of wreck or ruin."[15]

Bérard's main objection to what he takes to be an interpolation is grounded in his rejection of the fantastical elements of the magical Phaeacian ships. The line Joyce glosses calls Alcinous "*l'interpolateur*" who refers to the magical ships that are, in the translation of Butcher and Lang, "swift as the flight of a bird, or a thought" (according to Athena in Book 7).[16] The ships, Bérard concludes, are real and their ports can be discovered. He uses the etymology of Scheria to consider the possibility, active since Thucydides, that the island was Corfu. Bérard's premise that the *Odyssey* emerged from a material connection to actual maritime geography depends on rejecting these lines of Alcinous. In so doing, he defends his vision of the *Odyssey*'s attachment to material reality and topography, a vision that suited Joyce's vision of the vital and complex connection between literature and lived experience.

"Scylla and Charybdis" scrutinizes the collective reading practices of the men in the Library and critiques their tendencies toward abstraction, detachment, and sentimentality. Stephen voices the episode's skepticism about sentimentality most clearly in his epigrammatic telegram to Buck: "*The sentimentalist is he who would enjoy without incurring the immense debtorship for a thing done*" (*U* 9.550–1). As Gifford explains, this statement, from George Meredith's *The Ordeal of Richard Feverel* (1859) is followed by, "It is a happy . . . a happy pastime and an important science to the timid, the idle, and the heartless: but a damning one to them who have anything to forfeit" (*UA* 226). The conflicts about reading undergirding "Scylla and Charybdis" make visible the role the Phaeacians play in the *Odyssey*'s own project of defining proper and improper responses to epic song. As Stephen defines it here, audiences may be divided into two categories: the heartless and idle, who enjoy sentimentality as a happy pastime, and those with something to lose, who understand the power and the pain of art. Both kinds of audiences are present on the Homeric island of the Phaeacians.

The Life of Homer's Phaeacians

By having a Theosophist Revivalist admire an idealized version of the Phaeacians, *Ulysses* invites us to return to the Phaeacians to identify their function and limits as an audience. Scheria bears special importance in Homer's *Odyssey* as the space where Odysseus must earn his long-sought *nostos* so he can return to his identity as the King of Ithaca, husband of Penelope, and father of Telemachus. The most extended internal narrative in the *Odyssey* occurs on Scheria, when Odysseus recounts his adventures to a Phaeacian audience overseen by Alcinous and Arete. As characters, the Phaeacians are rife with contradictions, which can be seen in the lack of critical consensus about them. Although the Phaeacians have been viewed as the epitome of civilized humanity—a welcome relief from Odysseus's encounters with gods and monsters—their society and their history undermine their humanity.[17] As Jenny Strauss Clay argues, the Phaeacians are actually as distant from humanity as the Cyclopes are. They are, in fact, related to the Cyclopes via Poseidon (who is the father of Polyphemus and the grandfather of Alcinous). Scheria is also a land of rich abundance and pleasure. Their magical ships cross the seas without pilot and without hardships. Their ease in sailing forms an effective contrast with the long-suffering Odysseus, whose humanity is in part defined by his capacity to endure suffering on his long journey home. They are, on one hand, ideal hosts who embody the central virtues of hospitality, but as Steve Reece and others show, they also commit an astonishing number of violations of the codes of hospitality: Alcinous and Arete leave Odysseus in a heap of ashes for an extended period of time until they are reprimanded into inviting him in, Laodamas responds to Odysseus' tears by inviting him to participate in athletic contests, and Euryalus taunts Odysseus.[18]

Rather than trying to resolve these contradictions, I wish to question how they function in the *Odyssey*'s portrayal of the Phaeacians as the epic's most important embedded audience and more specifically how the Phaeacian scenes offer us a glimpse of the *Odyssey*'s modeling of proper responses to epic songs. As Robert Rabel argues, "The behavior of good audiences perhaps offers us a mirror in which we can glimpse our responsibilities as listeners to the song of the *Odyssey*."[19] Bruce Louden sees the Phaeacian audience as stand-ins for the external audience and identifies the Phaeacians as a "timeless, idealized audience."[20] Alcinous, he claims, is "almost a Platonic ideal of an epic audience: isolated, almost outside of the human-time continuum, yet eagerly appreciative of good narrative, indulgent, and more than generous to a narrator."[21] Doherty agrees that the Phaeacians are a privileged audience, but she is careful to note the gendered differences within the Phaeacian audience and to point out their naivete. A Joycean reading of the *Odyssey* would be attentive to the ways Homer's epic takes pains to invite its external audience to scrutinize the fantasy of a timeless, idealized song and audience—such scrutiny suggests that the Phaeacians illustrate the seductions of epic performances. If they serve as a model of how the *Odyssey*'s external audience should receive the epic, then that model is conveyed at least partly via a negative example of what not to do.

The Phaeacians are distant not only from the human world but also from the underlying ideology of the epic tradition as it defines what it means to be human. Both Homeric epics convey (from different angles) a world where men strive to earn *kleos* (imperishable glory). Both present and then complicate an ideology that requires that men die a noble battlefield death to earn an immortal name, but both also foreground suffering as central to the human experience. The Phaeacians have no experience with suffering or with war beyond presuming that war exists to offer their bard something to sing about to bring them pleasure. As Alcinous tells Odysseus, "The gods / devised and measured out this devastation, / to make a song for those in times to come" (O 8.578–80).[22] Stephen Dedalus's description of a "sentimentalist" as "one who would enjoy without incurring the immense debtorship for a thing done" applies to a Phaeacian audience that views human suffering as a source of aesthetic pleasure that costs them nothing. The *Odyssey* shares Joyce's concern for a relationship between art and life that makes room for a full range of human emotions and experiences.

The three songs of Demodocus establish the sharp contrasts between Odysseus and the Phaeacians in their responses to epic narratives. Demodocus, a blind singer often taken to be a stand-in for the poet of the *Odyssey*, begins his performance with a call to the Muses in a way that establishes his special relationship to them. What follows is a description of his song, which might be taken as an alternate *Iliad*:[23]

... They all
took food. When they were satisfied, the Muse
prompted the bard to sing of famous actions,
an episode whose fame has touched the sky:
Achilles; and Odysseus' quarrel—
how at a splendid sacrificial feast,
they argued bitterly, and Agamemnon
was glad because the best of the Achaeans
were quarreling ...

(*O* 8.71–9)[24]

As Yoav Rinon observes, the poet takes eight lines to describe the song and thirteen to describe the various reactions to the song. The audience of the *Odyssey*, therefore, is asked to evaluate the audience's reactions.[25] Further, Ronan argues that because we only hear a brief description of the song, there is "therefore a crucial difference between the information conveyed to Demodocus' narratees and that acquired by the narratees of the poet of the *Odyssey*."[26] The *Odyssey* reinforces a boundary between its audience and that of Demodocus and thus opens a distance for the audience of the *Odyssey* to scrutinize the reactions of both Odysseus and the Phaeacians. While the Phaeacians delight in the song, Odysseus weeps, we presume, because this story recalls his own painful past. Irene de Jong identifies this moment as intense metafiction that models for the external audience the expected mode of engagement: "Like the narrator, [members of the external audience] are not personally involved in the events of the story, and this may suggest a response similar to that of the Phaeacians: pure delight. And yet, the Homeric narrative style is implicitly, but unmistakably, aimed at arousing engagement and compassion."[27] In the absence of such compassion and engagement, Phaeacian pleasure depends on detachment—they maintain aesthetic detachment from the stories they hear in part because they presume their permanent distance from them. Demodocus's second song affirms this contrast—the story about Aphrodite, Ares, and Hephaestus uniformly pleases Odysseus and the Phaeacians, none of whom have any personal investment in it.

However, the third story complicates the easy separation between involved versus detached audiences suggested in the first two stories. As a prelude to his own story, Odysseus asks Demodocus to sing the story of the Trojan Horse, a story that has already been told in the *Odyssey* by Menelaus, who told it to disrupt and critique Helen's memory of Troy.[28] Demodocus tells his account of the Trojan Horse because Odysseus has prompted him to do so in a very specific way:

> You are wonderful, Demodocus!
> I praise you more than anyone; Apollo,
> or else the Muse, the child of Zeus, has taught you.
> You tell so accurately what the Greeks
> achieved, and what they suffered, there at Troy,
> as if you had been there, or hear about it
> from somebody who was. So sing the story
> about the Wooden Horse, which Epeius
> built with Athena's help. Odysseus
> dragged it inside and to the citadel,
> filled up with men to sack the town. If you
> can tell that as it happened, I will say
> that you truly are blessed with inspiration.
>
> (*O* 8.487–99)

Odysseus defines the shape of Demodocus's song that follows as well as its meaning—the song is about Odysseus's stratagem, the product of his *metis*, cunning. In his praise for Demodocus, Odysseus also reflects his belief that the value of poetry rests in its capacity to depict events vividly and accurately so that the audience can experience the event vicariously through the song.

Alcinous notes Odysseus's bard-like qualities when he tells him that he "sounded like a skillful poet" (*O* 11. 369).[29] For his story to be successful, Odysseus knows that the Phaeacians must become participants in it and must take on suffering and danger to do so. Odysseus's story acts as a kind of Trojan Horse for the Phaeacians, who do not seem fully aware of the implicit danger his story poses to them.

As Simon Goldhill argues, "What is told, how it is told, and to whom it is told is a thematic concern of the tale of the *Odyssey*." Alcinous is a limited audience in part because he fails to contend with what Goldhill calls the "essential duplicitousness" of language that is central to the *Odyssey*, which foregrounds "the manipulations, disguises, fictions that language can effect."[30] Glen Most argues that the message of all of Odysseus's stories is "let me go home now," to which I would add that the unfolding scene on Scheria suggests that the message of Odysseus's performance is also "take me home now."[31] Odysseus must convince his audience not merely to let him go, but rather to sacrifice their positions as the story's detached observers by becoming crucial, imperiled participants in it.

Alcinous hints at the threat Odysseus might pose to the safety of the Phaeacian people when he mentions the magical ships of the Phaeacians and recalls the prophecy told to him by his father:

> [Phaeacians] have no fear of damages or loss.
> But I once heard Nausithous, my father,
> say that Poseidon hates us for the help
> we give to take our guests across the sea,
> and that one day a ship of ours would suffer
> shipwreck on its return; a mighty mountain
> would block our town from sight. So Father said.
> Perhaps the god will bring these things to pass
> or not, as is his will . . .
>
> (*O* 8.563–72)

As I already noted, Joyce was interested in the fact that Bérard dismisses these lines as an interpolation because, he argues, it would not make sense for Alcinous to recall this right before Odysseus put into motion the narrative that would bring the prophecy to fruition. However, this "interpolation" intensifies the self-consciousness of the Phaeacian scene—it reaffirms Alcinous's sense of detachment from danger, suffering, and narrative. It also reaffirms his sense that suffering comes from the gods without human agency.

When Alcinous recalls his father's prophecy before he knows Odysseus's identity, he is preparing the *Odyssey*'s external audience to participate in the immediate work of memory demanded by the prophecy's fulfillment. After the Phaeacians deposit Odysseus on Ithacan shores, Alcinous remembers the prophecy and uses almost the same phrasing to describe it. Although Bérard rejects this repetition, I think it plays an important role in framing the Phaeacian response to epic stories—Odysseus has shown them that their sense of detachment from the world of suffering as told in stories was misguided and illusory. Alcinous's second recitation of the prophecy as it is happening illustrates his new understanding of the operation of both his history and Odysseus's story on the Phaeacian people. The external audience, therefore, would come to recognize in Alcinous a reader who has come to terms with stories after recognizing his part in them.

The Phaeacians are one of many examples that undermine twentieth-century theoretical approaches to the Homeric epics (such as those by Bakhtin, Lukacs, and Auerbach) that emphasize their totalized, finalized worldview. Such approaches have contributed to a critical sensibility outside of classical studies that has tended to view the Homeric epics as a relatively straightforward backdrop for comparatively complex modern narratives. The fate of the Phaeacians is left explicitly open in a way that draws attention to itself. The *Odyssey* drops the Phaeacians altogether as they pray to Poseidon to take pity on them and not pile a mountain over Scheria. The transition from Scheria to Ithaca is striking:

> So [Alcinous] spoke, and they were afraid and made bulls ready.
> So these leaders of the [Phaeacians] and men of counsel
> Among their people made prayer to the lord Poseidon,
> Standing around the altar. But now great Odysseus wakened
> From sleep in his own fatherland, and he did not know it . . .
>
> (O 13.185–9)[32]

It seems symbolically appropriate here for the Phaeacians to be frozen mid-action as they await their fate, which might include being buried by a mountain, being turned into a kind of grotesque monument of themselves. We may assume that Poseidon probably won't bury Scheria with a mountain because Zeus told him not to, but the framing of the end of the Phaeacian story seems to underline its indeterminacy. The caesura in line 188 abruptly abandons their story and moves to Odysseus on Ithaca, as if to emphasize that they no longer have a role in this story.[33] The fate of the Phaeacians remains a persistently unanswered question in the *Odyssey*, one that makes visible the cost of Odysseus's *nostos* and the requisite silences of a narrative centered on a single hero.

"I am not a character in fiction. I am a living being": Becoming Joyce's fiction

Ulysses and the *Odyssey* feature audiences who wish to maintain aesthetic distance from stories and who nevertheless are drawn into the stories they hear. In fact, both narratives literalize this conflict in ingenious and telling ways. Early on in his performance of his Shakespeare theory, Stephen tells himself, "Local colour. Work in all you know. Make them accomplices," thus articulating his intention to involve and implicate his audience in the unfolding of his story (*U* 9.158). As is well known, Joyce had a famously antagonistic relationship with at least some of his constructed audiences, which is perhaps best exemplified when he asked his brother Stanislaus to hand deliver copies of his scathing broadside "The Holy Office" around Dublin to the targets of the poem's criticism. Stephen adapts images from *Hamlet* to conceptualize an antagonistic model of language, telling himself early on, "They list. And in the porches of their ears I pour" (*U* 9.465). Likewise, when he contemplates his Aristotelian position in relation to his audience, he imagines that he will "unsheathe [his] dagger definitions," which adapts Hamlet's own metaphor of antagonistic speech when he thinks of Gertrude's betrayal and determines to "speak daggers to her but use none" (III.ii.379).[34] Stephen extends Hamlet's faith in the potentially destructive power of language and in the capacity for art to draw their audiences into the performance, as Hamlet does with the play within the play, which he uses to trap Claudius.[35] *Ulysses* extends this notion of literature as a trap by consuming the very audiences who presume their distance from literature.

Even though the plot cannot vindicate Stephen on June 16, 1904, we see the process by which he transforms this moment into "grist" for his mill and asserts his inner imaginative power over his fellow Dubliners as they assert social power over him. Early on in the episode, the stylistic play is relatively muted and seems focused mostly on asserting rhythm and syntax as concentrated characterizing devices, as seen in the characterization of Lyster's walk ("He came a step a sinkapace forward on neatsleather creaking and a step backward a sinkapace on the solemn floor") and in the staccato rhyme that introduces Mr. Best ("Mr Best entered, tall, young, mild, light. He bore in his hand … a notebook, new, large, clean, bright" [*U* 9.74–5]). These characterizations establish a pattern that comes to full fruition later in the episode as characterizing devices assert a kind of authorial power over the men.

The transition between this muted characterizing mode and the explosion of stylistic play at the end of the episode occurs when Buck enters. Buck's presence strengthens Stephen's sense of exclusion and his antagonism. After

Buck's entrance, the episode includes a brief musical score and then begins to play much more forcefully with the identities of all of the characters except for Stephen. In a discussion of Shakespeare leaving Ann Hathaway his second-best bed, for example, the following lines show the blurring of the boundary between dialogue and narration:

> —It is clear there were two beds, a best and a secondbest, Mr Secondbest Best said finely.
> —*Separatio a mensa et a thalamo,* bettered Buck Mulligan and was smiled on.
> —Antiquity mentions famous beds, Second Eglinton puckered, bedsmiling.
>
> (*U* 9.714–8)

Stephen's imagination appropriates and stylizes the speech of Mr. Best, Buck, and John Eglinton. More extremely, as Stephen talks about why Shakespeare's name "is dear to him," he turns the dialogue into a play. Stephen's name remains stable (as does Mr. Best's), while he runs together and reverses "MAGEEGLINJOHN," "BUCKMULLIGAN," "QUAKERLYSTER" in the framing of the play's dialogue (*U* 9.924; 9.900; 9.906; 9.918). He thus undermines the safety of the detachment his audience presumes they have and appropriates them for his fiction, subjecting their identities to his imaginative follies.

Of course, this kind of appropriation exposes the very mechanism by which Joyce generates fiction out of reality in a way that blurs the boundary between the two. As Norris argues, "Scylla and Charybdis" is "a high-risk extra-textual maneuver for Joyce himself. The contemporary 1922 reader of *Ulysses* familiar with Irish literary and cultural history might have been startled to find that characters in the episode included quite well-known living Irish *literati*."[36] Perhaps his greatest revenge on these members of the Dublin literati is that most of them are now remembered primarily as characters in Joyce's novel, particularly by readers who read as they do, with no concern for the biographical and historical contexts of the works they read. By transforming real people into fiction, Joyce settles the score and proves their theory of detached reading to be wrong. Richard Ellmann gives us a sense of how they eventually responded to being transformed into fictional characters:

> When the British Broadcasting Company was preparing to present a long program on Joyce, its representatives went to Dublin and approached Richard Best, sometime director of the National Library, to ask him to participate in a radio interview. "What makes you come to me?" he asked.

"What makes you think I have any connection with this man Joyce?" "But you can't deny your connection," said the men of the BBC. "After all, you're a character in *Ulysses*." Best drew himself up and retorted, "I am not a character in fiction. I am a living being."

(*JJ* 337)[37]

It is a fitting postscript to the conflicts about reception circulating in the National Library that Joyce's readers become aware of Mr. Best's objections to being treated as a fictional character by reading Ellmann's biography of Joyce, precisely the sort of contextual study that Joyce's fictional version of Best might reject. Joyce's fiction might strive to serve as a "nicely polished looking glass" or as a "sandblast" that leaves behind a "burnt up field" or as any number of other things, but it sharply critiques the notion that a story is an object of study hermetically sealed off from its author or its actual readers (*SL* 90; *SL* 241).

Gendering Reception in the Classical Tradition

The attention to reception underwriting both the *Odyssey* and *Ulysses* depends on each work's commitment to a notion of literature as transformative for its audiences. The men in the Library and the Phaeacians fail as audiences because they presume they cannot be personally changed by stories. The *Odyssey* depicts the transformative power of epics in the scene where Demodocus tells the story of the Wooden Horse and Odysseus responds:

Odysseus was melting into tears;
his cheeks were wet with weeping, as a woman
weeps, as she falls to wrap her arms around
her husband, fallen fighting for his home
and children. She is watching as he gasps
and dies. She shrieks a clear high wail, collapsing
upon his corpse. The men are right behind.
They hit her shoulders with their spears and lead her
to slavery, hard labor, and a life
of pain. Her face is marked with her despair.
In that same desperate way, Odysseus
was crying.

(*O* 8.521–32)

This example is what Helene P. Foley has called a "reverse simile," which suggests a "sense of identity between people in different social and sexual roles and a loss of stability, an inversion of the normal."[38] Odysseus's impulse to cry has been subject to some critical scrutiny, given his failure to cry at other key moments in the epic.[39] The context of performance on Scheria suggests that Odysseus is illustrating for the epic's external audience the power of narrative at precisely the moment when he himself will assume that power by becoming the narrator. Odysseus's wartime history was confined by the polarizing logics of gender and culture—he fought in the war in part because of a masculine code of honor that compelled him to defend the honor of the Achaeans. The poet here demonstrates the capacity of poetry to erode the distinctions of war by turning a victorious man into a defeated woman via transformative pathos.[40] The poet's language claims primacy for its own expressive power over both Odysseus's cunning and the masculine force demanded in battle.

Stephen's gendered theory of art emphasizes the transformative power of literature in an extended analogy that aligns the masculine with the feminine and reality with art:

> As we, or mother Dana, weave and unweave our bodies ... from day to day, their molecules shuttled to and fro, so does the artist weave and unweave his image. And as the mole on my right breast is where it was when I was born, though all my body has been woven of new stuff time after time, so through the ghost of the unquiet father the image of the unliving son looks forth.
>
> (*U* 9.376–81)

Although this analogy ends with the masculine artist and the father/son relation, it begins with women—Dana, Penelope (as the weaver), and presumably, for a moment, Stephen, who aligns himself with women through his use of the first-person plural pronoun. Engaging with the notion of feminine creativity leads Stephen to confront the new, the "possibilities of the possible as possible: things not known: what name Achilles bore when he lived among women" (*U* 9.349–51). At this moment, the "thing not known" is an alternate, non-Homeric version of the past when the warrior hero, disguised as a girl, lived on Skyros among women. This gesture toward a feminine history of Achilles supports Stephen's theories more generally in the Library, when he argues that a reading of Shakespeare must keep Ann Hathaway in view to an exclusively male audience who would prefer a version of history in which Ann

Hathaway "died, for literature at least, before she was born" (*U* 9.216). "Scylla and Charybdis" articulates a model of reading that reinscribes the feminine, the body, the actual, and the historical into the interpretive act.

"Scylla and Charybdis" focuses its attention, in large part, on how men see women in art and in the world. Bloom's brief appearance in "Scylla and Charybdis" establishes his distinctive way of approaching women in classical art. When Buck sees Bloom, he aligns him with the classical world by calling him "Greeker than the Greeks" (*U* 9.614–5). He tells Stephen and the others that he saw Bloom with his "pale Galilean eyes" fixed upon the "mesial groove" of the Venus Kallipyge at the National Museum of Dublin (*U* 9.615–6). This statue is one of many copies of Praxiteles's original statue, which is dated approximately 360 BC; although the original is lost, many Roman copies exist.[41] As Valérie Bénéjam notes, this statue is the first well-known female nude in Greek art and, as such, it shocked its audiences. This Venus, she argues, is:

> aware of the spectator, but she does not seem to mind. Thus she partakes of the image of both the goddess and the courtesan. Furthermore, if you approach the statue from the direction to which her gaze is directed, her left arm is still holding her tunic (a clear acknowledgment that Praxiteles had for the first time completely undressed the goddess), and the other arm does not obstruct the viewer's gaze: her body is completely open and defenseless. The right hand tries to cover her genitals, but the gesture directs the viewer's attention towards them instead of concealing them.[42]

This statue is a Roman copy of a lost Greek original that emphasizes its own exposure of the female body. One of the reasons why this statue created so much controversy is that it was widely known that the artist used a real woman as his model, so he was not only revealing divine female beauty, but also real, human beauty. Given the early date of composition of "Scylla and Charybdis," this moment offers a glimpse of Joyce's early reading of the Greek tradition, when he had yet to work out a stable theory of intertextual relation. The Venus Kallipyge emerges as an early symbol of *Ulysses*, which defines itself as a copy of a Greek original and which is remembered for the controversy it stirred up by its revelation of, among other things, the female body and female sexuality.

The figure of Venus recurs in Joyce's writing at moments of intense self-consciousness that seem to signal an engagement with the classical as a site of making visible the human body and the entire range of its experiences. In *Portrait*, when Stephen articulates his aesthetic theory, Lynch tells him about the time he wrote his name on the "backside of the Venus of Praxiteles in the Museum" (*P* 180). Here, at a moment when Stephen and Bloom encounter one another, the Venus appears as a self-reflexive object. Later, in "Nausicaa," Bloom thinks of his recent masturbatory encounter with Gerty and wonders, "Did she know what I? Course. Like a cat sitting beyond a dog's jump. Women never meet one like that Wilkins in the high school drawing a picture of Venus with all his belongings on show" (*U* 13.908–10). In these instances, a mode of eroticized engagement and illicit writing intersect at the figure of Venus. Although Buck assumes that Bloom's intentions in the Museum are purely lurid, we know from Bloom's thoughts in "Lestrygonians" that he is there because he admires beauty and wonders about the relationship between the statue as art and the real human body. More specifically, as he considers the biological processes of eating and excretion, he wonders if the statue has an anal opening (*U* 8.928–32). Bloom's genuine curiosity about the female body enables *Ulysses* to recontextualize it in reality and in art.

Scapegoating and Stasis in the Reception of Classical Women

The moment when Buck recounts Bloom's encounter with the Venus statue in "Scylla and Charybdis" serves as a prelude to the episode's attention to how readers see women in the classical tradition, an issue that remains important in the twenty-first century. In November 2017, Emily Wilson became the first female translator to publish a full translation in English of Homer's *Odyssey*.[43] That same month, she launched a Twitter account devoted primarily to discussing Homer and issues of translation. When she entered the Twittersphere, she entered a virtual space where the #metoo hashtag had just gone viral globally on social media with women sharing accounts of their experiences of rape and sexual assault. On multiple occasions, Wilson used Twitter as a platform to consider the relevance of the Homeric epics to the representation of sexual violence in the ancient and contemporary worlds. For example, in tweets posted on International Women's Day, she notes that she is thinking of the "murdered slave women in the *Odyssey*"—even though they are a "poetic construct," they nevertheless stand for millions of silenced, abused, and murdered women "in history and now."[44] Interviews with Wilson inevitably focus on her status as the first woman to translate the *Odyssey*. She typically seizes the occasion to consider the ideological implications of such lines of questioning, noting in one interview that it is "interesting that [she's] seen as the only translator of the *Odyssey* who has a gender identity" and that perhaps it would have been relevant to note the gender identity of male translators. For example, she notes:

> ... when earlier English translators have added in misogynistic language that definitely doesn't correspond to the Greek, reviewers have never ever, as far as I can tell, called them out on it. For instance, when Telemachus, in Book 22, says that he will hand the women who "slept with the suitors," Richmond Lattimore uses the word "creatures"; Robert Fitzgerald uses the word "sluts," as does Stanley Lombardo; Stephen Mitchell has him say they "whored" with the suitors; Robert Fagles, an expansive translator, has "sluts" and "whores" both.[45]

Wilson concludes that such language is not inevitable and that what is notable is that "no reviewer seemed to think it even deserved a mention, and it's interesting that this kind of thing is not described as a 'male viewpoint,' at least not in most current press coverage of male writers. All that needs to start changing, right about yesterday or the day before."[46] Wilson's *Odyssey* helps foreground an intersection among ideas of the classics, women, language, and authority that was important for Joyce and remains important for us.

As Lillian Doherty has shown, conflicts between male and female audiences run through the *Odyssey*.[47] One of the first mortal conversations that happens in the *Odyssey* occurs when the grief-stricken Penelope implores the Ithacan bard to sing a song about something other than the warriors who returned home from Troy. Telemachus's first act is to silence her and send her away. The song Penelope wanted to hear remains as a potential, but unrealized song in the space of the *Odyssey*. When Telemachus journeys to the palace of Menelaus and Helen, he and we hear two competing accounts of the fall of Troy. Helen first tells her story of the moment in the Trojan War when she recognized Odysseus through his disguise and aided him in secret. Menelaus responds by offering a competing account of Troy, one that paints Helen in a much less flattering light:

You came there too, some spirit who desired
to glorify the Trojans urged you on . . .
Three times you went around the hollow belly,
touching the hiding place, and calling on
us Greeks by name; you put on different voices
for each man's wife. Then I and Diomedes
and good Odysseus, inside the horse,
heard you call out to us, and we two wanted
to go out, or to answer from in there.
Odysseus prevented us from going.

(O 4.274–84)

Menelaus gets the final word in this story for the moment, as all of the men fall asleep, having drunk the wine Helen mixed with Egyptian narcotics to take away their pain. This moment leaves open the status of Helen's story in relation to Menelaus's, which attempts to override hers. The *Odyssey* shows that he only partly succeeds because this story is told again. The audience of the *Odyssey* returns to a version of this story when Odysseus asks Demodocus, the Phaeacian bard, to sing the story of the Wooden Horse. Demodocus's story emphasizes the wile of Odysseus in hatching this plot without mentioning Helen or her supposed treachery. Helen remains a target of criticism throughout the epic, as seen, for example, in the *Nekuia* when Odysseus speaks with the shade of Agamemnon, who describes Clytemnestra's treachery. "Curse her!" Odysseus cries out, "Zeus has always brought / disaster to the house of Atreus / through women. Many were lost for Helen, / and Clytemnestra formed this plot against you / when you were far away" (*O* 11.435–439). Helen slides into Odysseus's speech almost as an afterthought as he blames the plight of the Achaeans on women. In this way, the *Odyssey* anticipates a script that would replay over millennia about Helen as the *femme fatale* and destroyer of men.

Joyce paid attention to the history of Helen. For example, in the notes he took to prepare for his *Hamlet* lectures in 1912, he copied the entirety of the apostrophe to Helen in Marlowe's *Doctor Faustus* (the passage that refers to her "face that launch'd a thousand ships / And burnt the topless towers of Ilium"). This static image of Helen as the destroyer of men is an oft-repeated trope, seen in Joyce's lifetime, for example, in Yeats' poems (e.g. "No Second Troy" and "Leda and the Swan"). In his reading notes on Walter Leaf's *Troy: A*

Study in Homeric Geography, he noted, "Herodotus opens history with Phenician version of rape of Helen."[48] Joyce's references to Helen draw attention to the way such static tropes continue to circulate in modern culture. Although Helen appears on the Linati schema twice, she is not a character, and she does not participate in the plot. Rather, she is a classical figure about whom the male characters speak.

The text's performance of allusions to Helen seems to activate a vast tradition dedicated to reprising or rethinking her role in the myth of the Trojan War.[49] As Mihoko Suzuki has recently argued in a study of Helen across literary history, "the representation of woman, as the motivating force and stated goal of epic narrative, becomes a crucial locus for the poet's assertion of difference from both literary and political authority," a description that aptly describes the context of Joyce's self-conscious representation of classical women.[50] The novel's depiction of Helen illustrates the dull, easy, and damaging mode of classical memory operating in the early twentieth century, what Stephen dubbed "the dull ease of the mind" in "Nestor." Near the end of "Nestor," Mr. Deasy's comments on Helen prop up and affirm his more general tendencies toward misogyny, anti-Semitism, and a world view that depends on scapegoating. He tells Stephen: "A woman brought sin into the world. For a woman who was no better than she should be, Helen, the runaway wife of Menelaus, ten years the Greeks made war on Troy" (*U* 2.390–2). This sets up his condemnation of other women, including Kitty O'Shea.

Later references to Helen show more clearly on a micro level how easily this kind of logic becomes affirmed and internalized. In "Aeolus," when Stephen hands over Mr. Deasy's letter, he thinks of Deasy's wife and remembers his position on Helen almost verbatim: "A woman brought sin into the world. For Helen, the runaway wife of Menelaus, ten years the Greeks" (*U* 7.536–7) Later in "Aeolus," Professor MacHugh, the classicist, tells Stephen (after he has told his parable of the plums) that he reminds him "of Antisthenes . . . a disciple of Gorgias, the sophist. It is said of him that none could tell if he were bitterer against others or against himself. He was the son of a noble and a bondwoman. And he wrote a book in which he took away the palm of beauty from Argive Helen and handed it to poor Penelope" (*U* 7.1035–9).[51] This statement alludes to a text that has not survived in which Antisthenes argues that Penelope is more beautiful than Helen because her virtue makes her beautiful. What has survived is the work of Gorgias, who wrote an encomium to Helen, which used various rhetorical strategies to rehabilitate her image. One of his main arguments was that she was deceived by language, which is itself a master. If this is the case, he argues, then her flight with Paris is not her fault. Joyce's later addition of headings to "Aeolus" plays with this sense of language's power with the heading:

SOPHIST WALLOPS HAUGHTY HELEN SQUARE ON PROBOSCIS. SPARTANS GNASH MOLARS. ITHACANS VOW PEN IS CHAMP.

(*U* 7.1032–4)

This heading turns the conflict between Helen and Penelope into a sporting contest where both the pen and Penelope emerge as victors. The process of condensing history into this form also inevitably distorts that history through simplification and omission and causes the denigration of Helen. This heading draws our attention to the verbal form of this conflict, where language seems to have its own driving logic, where the alliteration of "haughty" and "Helen" almost seems self-evident and the pun between "Penelope" and "pen" brings to the surface a connection between Penelope and writing that will later be realized in the novel's final episode. Sound has a particular kind of associative power in this moment, as the professor's reference to Penelope evokes Stephen's recollection of "Penelope Rich," who was a well-known adulterer and the inspiration for a sonnet sequence by Sir Philip Sidney. The mention of Penelope creates an associative pun in Stephen's mind that evokes values that directly contradict the ideals of fidelity and patience typically associated with Penelope. *Ulysses* thus draws our attention to an intersection of language and thought that leads almost inevitably toward a hostile reading of women in the classical tradition, a reading that might be easily and unconsciously reproduced in contemporary society.

In "Scylla and Charybdis," during the discussion of Ann Hathaway's influence on Shakespeare's writing, John Eglinton finally becomes interested and notes that if he thought of her at all, he thought of her as a "Penelope stayathome," therefore not worthy of historical attention. Almost on cue, Stephen responds in ways that recycle and intensify the earlier characterizations of Helen and Penelope by saying, "—Antisthenes, pupil of Gorgias . . . took the palm of beauty from Kyrios Menelaus' brooddam, Argive Helen, the wooden mare of Troy in whom a score of heroes slept, and handed it to poor Penelope" (*U* 9.621–3). This begins an exposition of women who influenced Shakespeare and others in his circle, ending with Penelope Rich—a thought process that structurally repeats what Stephen earlier thought in "Aeolus." Stephen quotes himself, MacHugh, and Deasy directly and indirectly in this statement, in a way that intensifies rhetorical hostility against Helen, which is evident in his characterization of her as a "broodam" and as a "wooden mare of Troy." This last reference evokes the image of the Trojan Horse, the center of her narrative conflict with Menelaus. Stephen's addition of this image to this accumulating microtradition forming in the novel around Helen raises the question: What might it mean for Helen to be a Trojan Horse in *Ulysses*?

In one of his notebooks (Zurich notebook VIII.A.I.7), Joyce notes that Odysseus made a *zylinon alogon* (wooden animal).[52] This phrase, Schork notes, is clumsy but accurate—"The Greek prefix *a-* (not) is combined with the noun *logos* (word, speech, idea, reason, and so on) to designate a nonspeaking or nonthinking thing."[53] Helen functions precisely as a nonspeaking being in *Ulysses*—she is a classical female figure about whom the men in the novel think and speak. If, as Hugh Kenner argues, "language is the Trojan Horse by which the universe gets into the mind," then Helen as a figure about whom men speak exerts a kind of damaging potential.[54] The novel's men seem to infect one another with frozen images of Helen that retain much of their original phrasing while intensifying in contextual antagonism. In this, we might see her as a Trojan Horse in the same way Throwaway is—she is a signifier who accumulates characteristics and meanings that eventually threaten to explode into a kind of imaginative or actual violence. The circulation of the figure of Helen through various masculine spaces in the novel illustrates a damaging process of classical reception grounded in repetition.

Joyce's own deployment of female figures from classical literature depends on an ideology of transformation, not repetition. In Joyce's literary landscape, classical reception demands that readers become co-authors who recreate the images they receive—the act of reading coincides with an act of authorship. Reading women in the classical tradition was an essential activity in Joyce's development of *Ulysses*. Joyce's well-known comments on Bloom as a modern Odysseus show that, for the most part, this correspondence remained stable over the course of his work on *Ulysses*, but his reading of Penelope and classical women evolved over the course of his composition.[55] For example, the "Subject Notebook" at the National Library of Ireland—which captures some of Joyce's earliest specific work on the novel—contains a single entry under the heading "Homer": "Calypso=Penelope."[56] This entry is canceled, which means Joyce used it. In the earliest days of writing and conceptualizing the novel, Joyce's engagement with Homer shows his reconfiguration of Homer's goddesses and women. His process of reception, therefore, coincided with his process of writing. In a later notebook, Joyce wrote another tantalizing Penelopean equation from his reading of W.H. Roscher: "Penelope=Homer Philostratos," referring to a description of Penelope's weaving.[57] This note suggests that Joyce was reconceptualizing Penelope not only as unfaithful but also as an artist with agency—both come to fruition in Molly Bloom.

As the Homeric artist who unweaves her creation each night only to start again the next day, Penelope is the emblematic figure of the dynamic artist who avoids static representation. For this reason, it is not surprising the she is the one character in the *Odyssey* who voices a view of Helen that remains independent of the virtually identical hostile depictions circulating among the epic's men.[58] When Odysseus passes Penelope's test of the bed, she responds in a distinctive way:

> The gods have made us suffer: they refused
> to let us stay together and enjoy
> our youth until we reached the edge of age
> together. Please forgive me, do not keep
> bearing a grudge because when I first saw you,
> I would not welcome you immediately.
> I felt constant dread that some bad man
> would fool me with his lies. There are so many
> dishonest, clever men. That foreigner
> would never have gotten Helen into bed,
> if she had known the Greeks would march to war
> and bring her home again. It was a goddess
> who made her do it, putting in her heart
> the passion that first caused my grief as well.

(O 23.213–26)

Penelope emerges as a figure of an ideal reader in the *Odyssey*—she understands the deceptive power of language and navigates it successfully. This mode of interpretation precedes her empathetic engagement with Helen, one that leads her to understand how Helen's history might have unfolded differently. To put it as Stephen Dedalus might have, when Penelope thinks of Helen, she "ponders things that were not ... what might have been: possibilities of the possible as possible: things not known."

Transforming the Authority of Classical Women

Joyce's research played an important role in his self-conscious re-writing of the authority of women in the classical tradition. In particular, Samuel Butler's *The Authoress of the* Odyssey offered Joyce a way of conceptualizing Homer as a woman. Butler used topographical suggestions and depictions of women in the *Odyssey* to conclude that its author was a teenage girl from Trapani. More specifically, he suggested, its author was the prototype for Nausicaa, something that Joyce certainly picks up in the "Nausicaa" episode of *Ulysses* in its emphasis on Gerty's various acts of authorship.[59]

Ulysses suggests that Joyce took seriously Butler's arguments about female authorship—if not literally than at least conceptually—as well as his arguments about women. Michael Seidel points to the potential significance of Butler when he compared Butler's arguments about Homer to Stephen's about Shakespeare in "Scylla and Charybdis": "With a set of Homeric theories resembling those of Stephen Dedalus's on Shakespeare, Butler combines a few narrative facts, many local and topographical details, and a great deal of raw wit to place the authoress of the *Odyssey*, the young Nausicaa, in a small town on a west coast of Sicily."[60] I would extend this point to argue that "Scylla and Charybdis" signals an indebtedness to Butler in its depiction of Stephen's rhetorical stance against a hostile audience, its connection between Homer and Shakespeare, and even its language. Butler recruits Shakespeare to dismantle the oral theory of Friedrich Wolf, who argued that the Homeric poems were composed orally by multiple authors: "Who would have thought of attacking Shakespeare's existence—for if Shakespeare did not write his plays he is no longer Shakespeare—unless men's minds had been unsettled by Wolf's virtual denial of Homer's?" Butler explicitly connects the legacies of Homer and Shakespeare in a way that helps create the conceptual foundation for

"Scylla and Charybdis," the novel's most self-conscious episode. Butler anticipates a stand-off with his classicist readers in the following way: "How can I expect Homeric scholars to tolerate theories so subversive of all that most of them have been insisting on for so many years? It is a matter of Homeric (for my theory affects Iliadic questions nearly as much as it does the "Odyssey") life and death for them or for myself. If I am right they have invested their reputation for sagacity in a worthless stock." Butler's sense of his argument as a zero-sum game with an audience invested in established ideas anticipates Stephen's understanding of the reception of his own theory by an audience he perceives as antagonistic to him. Butler ends this description of his battle with Homeric scholars by concluding, "They will be more than human, therefore, if they do not handle me somewhat roughly," a statement echoed by Mr. Best's "gentle" defense of Shakespeare: "Gentle Will is being roughly handled" (*U* 9.793).

Whereas Helen illustrates the circulation of static classical images in the modern imagination, Penelope carries the potential for radical reinvention into Joyce's novel. Butler argued for a version of Penelope that will seem familiar to readers of Joyce. He considers the extensive history starting with the *Telegony* that supposed that Penelope was in fact unfaithful and considers the pains the *Odyssey* takes to insist on her fidelity. He concludes, "The amount of caution with which she is credited is to some extent a gauge of the thickness of the coat of whitewash the writer considers necessary. In all Penelope's devotion to her husband there is an ever-present sense that the lady doth protest too much."[61] He reads the representation psychologically and concludes that this writer understood little about adult men, women, or sex. He concludes that the author wanted to "exalt her sex by showing how a clever woman can bring any number of men to her feet." He also concludes, "I know of no male writer who has attempted anything like it."[62] It is entirely possible that Joyce may have read such a statement as a challenge and that we might read Molly Bloom as a response to it.

Joyce's *Ulysses* began with the adaptation of a Homeric model of heroic ideology and it ended with a transferal of narrative agency to Molly. In this context, we can see the ways that engaging with the critical response to the women of Homer helped bolster the decision he described to Frank Budgen in December 1920: "I am going to leave the last word with Molly Bloom—the final episode Penelope being written through her thoughts and body Poldy being then asleep" (*SL* 274). He expanded on this decision in February 1921: "The last word (human, all too human) is left to Penelope. This is the indispensable countersign to Bloom's passport to eternity. I mean the last episode Penelope" (*SL* 278). Joyce's reading of the classical tradition helped him to shape a reading of the *Odyssey* that seems to have more in common with Wilson's reading than with the more general tradition of twentieth-century translation. In this, Joyce also seems to have anticipated the explosion of interest in recent decades in engaging the Homeric epics from a female perspective, which can be seen in the works of Margaret Atwood, Louise Glück, Madeline Miller, and many others. In Joyce's vision, the *Odyssey* reaches fulfillment not with simply a return to a woman marked as the end of adventure, but rather with an arrival at a female voice that is given authority and, finally, the last word. Molly Bloom's famous "yes I said yes I will Yes" itself engages in a repetition of affirmation, but the final, emphatic, capitalized "Yes" breaks the grammatical pattern and is, in the end, a moment of repetition made new.

Epilogue

The Pleasures of (Not) Reading Joyce and the Classics

In 2014, a year that saw the celebration of her debut novel, *A Girl Is a Half-Formed Thing*, Eimear McBride published a tribute to James Joyce. "Difficulty is subjective," McBride wrote, and "the demands a writer makes on a reader can be perceived as a compliment ... Joyce certainly compliments his readers in what he asks of them."[1] Reading Joyce turned McBride into a writer. She notes, "Joyce really set my universe on its end. Reading *Ulysses* changed everything I thought about language, and everything I understood about what a book could do."[2] As reading Joyce shaped McBride's sense of literature, reading and remaking the classics helped Joyce understand what a book could do. As I have argued, Joyce used Stephen Dedalus and prototypes of Stephen to argue for a versatile, invested model of classical reading. This model may be traced in multiple directions—to Bloom and Molly, who realize the ideals toward which Stephen strives; to *Finnegans Wake* as radical redefinition of the reading process; and to contemporary writers such as McBride who help us to think more expansively about Joyce beyond academic discussions of his work. As I will suggest, contemporary writers have offered radically personalized readings of Joyce that mirror his own readings of the classics and that share his sense of literature as embedded in and relevant to everyday experience.

Ulysses introduces Bloom as a voracious reader of the texts of everyday life—a letter from his daughter, an advertisement, and his wife's novel, which has fallen and is "sprawled against the bulge of the orangekeyed chamberpot," a fitting image of the easy assimilation of texts into the Blooms' household (*U* 4.329–30). Within the domestic sphere, Bloom displays his facility for successfully navigating the minute interpretive tasks of daily experience. When he hears a woman singing to the music of a dulcimer, he is quick to distinguish the seduction of the song from reality: "Probably not a bit like it really. Kind of stuff you read" (*U* 4.99). When he reads *Matcham's Masterstroke* in the outhouse, he enjoys it, noting that it begins and ends morally—moments later, it serves another purpose, when he uses it to wipe himself. After he experiences the intellectual pleasure of reading and an extremely quotidian use of the material text, he turns his thoughts to authorship. He envies the fact that the author was paid "three pounds, thirteen and six" for the story and considers writing one himself ("Might manage a sketch") (*U* 4.504–5, 518). He imagines that he might "invent a story" and remembers the time he "used to try jotting down on [his] cuff what [Molly] said dressing" (*U* 4.518–20). Unlike Stephen, who has yet to recognize the everyday as the site of his art, Bloom is prompted by his reading to consider how he might become an author of fiction grounded in his own daily life with Molly. He imagines signing the story "By Mr and Mrs L.M. Bloom," a suggestive byline that signals the collaborative shape of his imagined authorship as a way of blending his identity with Molly's. This moment reinforces the ways that reading in Joyce's literary universe is the first step of writing; both reading and writing offer the possibility of transformation and connection.

As a champion of the value of reading, Joyce has offered generations of writers a pathway to authorship through a transformative experience of reading his fiction. His influence on later writers is so profound that evaluating his impact on later classical reception as both a creative practice and a critical method requires understanding the more general landscape of his literary legacies. A trope in contemporary writing is the contemporary writer discovering his or her artistic identity through an intense, formative reading of Joyce. Derek Walcott's 1990 *Omeros* imaginatively travels to Dublin to address Joyce as "our age's Omeros, undimmed Master / and true tenor of the place!"[3] An early diary entry shows Walcott as a figure who very much resembles Stephen asking, as Stephen did in the library, when it will be his turn:

> Reading Joyce, you have, of course. Even Stephen. Son of a pastiche. Some article I read by whatshisnamenow, in a Life and Letters, yes, predicting that someday a new Ulysses willcomeforth out of these emerald, ethnic isles, and sure then he had put his finger on me. Imitation, imitation, when will I be me?[4]

Walcott's movement from "reading Joyce" to "when will I be me" neatly captures the model of classical reception that Joyce employed in his fiction as an engine of artistic and personal development. As if taking his cue from the style of "Scylla and Charybdis," Walcott opens a distance between himself and Joyce's academic readers, marked by the Joycean elision "whatshisnamenow." The lesson he took from reading Joyce, he argued in an interview, was that "one could come out of a depressed, depraved, oppressed situation and be defiant and creative at the same time."[5] Echoing Walcott's identification of Joyce's defiant creativity, Seamus Heaney notes that Joyce left "a loophole for the soul which others had found and followed through."[6] When Heaney's version of *Antigone* was opening at the Abbey Theatre in 2004, Eileen Battersby asked him, "Why have so many of Ireland's leading writers been drawn to reworking versions of classic works?" She noted that he smiled as he replied, "because classics endure." He continued by reflecting on the turbulence of recent decades of Irish political and social history and concluding that, "All these fundamental issues are plied with total clear-sightedness for the first time in the Greek classics. But that does not mean that the last word has been spoken."[7]

The reception of Joyce by later literary artists suggests the power of a set of versatile reading practices that are not limited to traditionally sanctioned academic readings. In a *New York Times* column commemorating Bloomsday in 2009, Colum McCann admitted that during a recent extended hospital stay, he read *Ulysses* cover to cover for the first time. He acknowledged, "I have been dipping into the novel for many years, reading the accessible parts, plundering the icing on the cake, but in truth I had never read it all in one flow." His use of the word "plundering" (however tongue in cheek) here suggests the illicit nature of a partial reading of Joyce's famous and famously difficult novel—the implication being that full credit is only given for finished readings. McCann's full reading led him to a surprising discovery—between the covers of *Ulysses*, he discovered himself and a way of thinking about the unknown history of his deceased grandfather. He concluded, "Sometimes one story can be enough for anyone: it suffices for a family, or a generation, or even a whole culture—but on occasion there are enormous holes in our histories, and we don't know how to fill them."[8]

This movement from a sheepish partial reading to a full reading that generates an intensive experience of self-discovery and an appreciation of the form and function of stories is echoed in Gabriel García Márquez's account of his history of reading Joyce. In his memoir, Márquez refers to his "other Bible": "It was, of course, James Joyce's *Ulysses*, which I read in bits and pieces and fits and starts until I lost all patience. It was premature brashness. Years later, as a docile adult, I set myself the task of reading it again in a serious way, and it not only was the discovery of a genuine world that I never suspected inside me, but it also provided invaluable technical help to me in freeing language and in handling time and structures in my books."[9] Joyce's influence on McCann and García Márquez was not immediate—they both abandoned reading *Ulysses* before embracing it years later with a renewed sense of purpose.

To evaluate the afterlife of Joyce's reception of the classics as part of his fiction's foregrounding of the value of reading, this chapter charts the tension between abandoning and embracing Joyce's fiction by reading *The Sixteenth of June* by Maya Lang and *Fun Home* by Alison Bechdel. These works extend Joyce's own model of classical engagement, which depends on experimentation and misreading, in the service of human connection, freedom, and self-discovery. A deeply self-conscious impulse undergirds the dynamic readings of Joyce and *Ulysses* at the center of *Fun Home* and *The Sixteenth of June*. Both employ something like a twenty-first century mythic method to organize their narratives in dialogue with the plot, characters, and themes of *Ulysses*. However, *Ulysses* is not merely present in both works as an exterior narrative scaffold, visible to us but not to the novel's characters. In both, characters are actively reading, pretending to have read, misreading, studying, celebrating, dismissing, attacking, ignoring, and talking about *Ulysses*. Lang's and Bechdel's characters interpret themselves and their lives in dialogue with Joyce's novel, and much as McCann and García Márquez did, they discover themselves as they read *Ulysses*.

Ulysses offers the means for raising questions about the purpose, value, and substance of reading in the twenty-first century. As Beth Blum observes, *Ulysses* has been particularly amenable to this kind of self-conscious interrogation, as it has served as a *"locus classicus* for questioning literature's real-world value; the daunting complexity of Joyce's narrative forces readers to articulate, perhaps even reconsider, the expectations they bring to literary texts."[10] *Fun Home* and *The Sixteenth of June* interrogate the limitations of conventional, academic reading processes that have both affirmed the canonical power of *Ulysses* and the classical tradition in which it participates and threatened to render them obsolete to and unread by twenty-first century readers. In different ways, both works experiment with a range of recuperative, affective, identificatory models of reading. They reject the *Ulysses* we thought we knew in order to propose alternative visions of the continued, urgent relevance of Joyce's work and the classics.

"For All Those Who Never Made it Through *Ulysses*": Maya Lang's *The Sixteenth of June*

The Sixteenth of June joins Declan Kiberd in rejecting *Ulysses* as a cultural symbol of prestige understood only by specialists. Although Lang does not explicitly allude to the classics, her work reimagines Joyce's classical project for contemporary audiences. *The Sixteenth of June* engages *Ulysses* at the level of form, narrative, language, themes, and characters. It features eighteen chapters, and each one includes at least one direct quotation from the corresponding episode of *Ulysses*—the quotations include statements seamlessly integrated into the novel's narrative and conscious references spoken by the novel's characters (Lang lists them on her author's website).[11] Lang has based her characters on *Ulysses*, but perhaps more importantly, some of her characters have, in Wildean fashion, self-consciously adapted Joycean identities. Michael Portman, a trader, hosts Philadephia's cultural elite at his annual Bloomsday party. His wife, the socialite June, pretends she has read *Ulysses*, "knowing that bonus points are awarded for obscurity" (*SJ* 175). Their children, Leopold and Stephen, distantly correspond to their Joycean counterparts—Leopold is a pragmatic, optimistic IT consultant and Stephen is a wayward graduate student writing a dissertation on modernist fiction as he grieves the death of his grandmother. He is also the only member of the family who has actually read *Ulysses* thoroughly (though he prefers Virginia Woolf). Rounding out the Joycean cast of characters is Leopold's fiancée, Nora; and Dedalus, the family golden retriever. The crucial presence of Nora as the novel's main protagonist suggests that the intertextual operations of *The Sixteenth of June* include not only the precursor text but also its larger biographical context. *The Sixteenth of June*'s intertextual engagement with *Ulysses* breaches the boundary between text and context and violates the New Critical ideal of aesthetic autonomy of which its characters are skeptical.

    The Sixteenth of June does more than just establish narrative, thematic, and character parallels with *Ulysses*—it explicitly evaluates the place of *Ulysses* and the mythology surrounding Joyce as an emblem of the cultural prestige of the classics in the twenty-first century. The novel's paratextual framing of *The Sixteenth of June* makes the reception of *Ulysses* an unmistakable critical problem. The novel's title refers not only to the day Leopold Bloom traversed Dublin but also the annual commemoration of Joyce's novel on Bloomsday. Lang highlights the social significance of reading *Ulysses* by dedicating *The Sixteenth of June* in the following way: "For all the readers who never made it through *Ulysses* (or haven't wanted to try)." By responding to the cultural currency one might gain by claiming to have climbed the intellectual equivalent of Everest, this novel introduces its own preoccupation with reading—what one reads (to read or not to read *Ulysses?*), how one reads, and why. A pair of epigraphs establish the novel's tension between reverence for and rejection of *Ulysses*. The first is from an NPR broadcast about the centenary celebration of Bloomsday in Dublin as a "unique literary event," a day-long Irish and global celebration of *Ulysses* by specialists, readers, fans, and non-readers. The second is from Virginia Woolf's diary: "The book is diffuse. It is brackish. It is pretentious. It is underbred, not only in the obvious sense, but in the literary sense. A first-rate writer ... respects writing too much to be tricky." This epigraph draws upon Woolf's criticism of Joyce's style and her rejection of Joyce's claims to writerly authority (as a "first-rate writer"). Stephen Portman voices the Woolfian critique of Joyce's influence running through *The Sixteenth of June* by noting the "literary acrobatics" in the contemporary novel and saying he is skeptical of writing that "tries too hard. Why can't writers just come out and say what they mean? Has sincerity gone out of style? I wonder if we've become too clever for our own good" (*SJ* 177). Although Lang's novel does not seem to endorse the snobbishness of Woolf's most caustic reactions to Joyce (only hinted at in the epigraph), it is invested in reanimating Woolf's early reading and returning us to a moment of cultural reception before June 16 acquired cultural significance, before *Ulysses* was, as Latham observes, "appropriated by the very cultural hierarchies of value it sought to contest."[12]

The readers inscribed in *The Sixteenth of June* enable the novel's critique of two different categories of readers: academic readers (best embodied by Stuart, Stephen's dissertation advisor) and culture snobs (primarily Michael and June Portman). The Portmans are possessive readers—they appropriate *Ulysses* as a symbol of refined aesthetic taste to enhance their image. Michael Portman made millions from the kind of derivatives-based short selling that brought the global economy to the brink of collapse in 2008. He brags about having studied *Ulysses* with Richard Ellmann at Harvard. He relishes the cumulative social capital granted to him by his experience with *Ulysses* at his Bloomsday parties. June plays along and pretends to have read *Ulysses*. She also hides her treasured copy of *When Harry Met Sally* behind the Godard and Truffaut DVDs on her shelf. By juxtaposing the Portmans' elaborate party preparations with their lack of knowledge of the book they celebrate, the novel interrogates the social commodification of *Ulysses*.

The Sixteenth of June also treats academic readers who approach the text without regard for its affective personal significance with skepticism. Stephen and his dissertation advisor Stuart are the only people at the party who have clearly made it all the way through *Ulysses*, but they have opposite responses to its difficulty. Stephen notes that, "No other writer thumbed his nose so flagrantly at the reader" (*SJ* 178). Claiming that "*Ulysses* was never meant to seduce us gently" and "there are challenges and wonders at every turn," Stuart defends its difficulty and its status as an intellectual Everest because, "We discover something meaningful in the climb precisely because it pushes us" (*SJ* 178). Moreover, Stuart is attracted by the encyclopedic, nearly prophetic quality of *Ulysses* as "the repository of everything" and notes that he finds "it magically relevant, as though Joyce anticipates all" (*SJ* 178).

Stephen refuses Stuart's claim that *Ulysses* is the "repository of everything" and responds, "But that's not what a book is supposed to do ... A book is a place to lose yourself and then find yourself once more. A book draws you into its world like a charming host. It should not make you regret the invitation" (*SJ* 178). Stuart foregrounds the prophetic power of *Ulysses* as a repository that knows more than its readers, but Stephen privileges the function of literature to invite a personally meaningful experience of self-discovery for its readers. For this reason, he is contemptuous of the Bloomsday party itself because of its shallow display of affection for an unread book. Standing beneath a custom-made banner reading "Yes I said yes I will Yes," Stephen tells Stuart:

> I sometimes think they're more interested in what *Ulysses* says about them than what it actually says. Our truest relationships to books is private. I love *Gatsby*. I love *Mrs. Dalloway*. But I would never throw a party for them. A party ends up celebrating not the book but its title ... Joyce fans can never

keep it to themselves. People who tell you that they love *Ulysses*—they wear it like it's a badge.

(*SJ* 176)

Stephen celebrates reading as an act that must be individuated, private, and based in fidelity to the text (and what it "actually says").

Although the novel mostly seems to agree with Stephen's perspective, it also is more generous in its presentation of the other partygoers who have not read *Ulysses* all the way through. The Bloomsday party implies the potential value of partial reading. Nora identifies with *Ulysses* and "wonders if they aren't so different from *Ulysses*" even though she never made it to the end of the novel (*SJ* 88). Stephen's father, another partial reader who indeed wears his love of *Ulysses* like a badge, unsettles Stephen's notion that a public celebration of *Ulysses* must be of necessity shallow. Adding to the conversation, Michael delivers a speech honoring his mother (whose funeral was that morning) and offering his own sense of how and why we read:

> ... literature provides comfort. We find solace in its pages. No one can say the right thing to me today; it is a day where words feel insufficient. But this book still speaks to me, after all this time. It always manages to reach me. And that is something worthy of being honored ... And so today we celebrate Bloomsday. We celebrate a book's ability to move us. We celebrate all that makes life worthy, all that makes us rise out of bed when rain and a funeral await. We affirm Molly's glorious 'Yes I said yes I will Yes.' We celebrate this together, and in that I take great comfort. Because when all else has passed, this book will remain.
>
> (*SJ* 194)

Michael takes comfort not only in the enduring value of *Ulysses* but also in a communal celebration of its affirmative, emotional power. This moment seems to clarify the book's dedication to readers who never made it all the way through Joyce's novel, who did not make it to the top of Everest. Taken in the context of the novel's Bloomsday party, that dedication is not a refusal or dismissal of *Ulysses*. Instead, the dedication questions the priority different kinds of snobbish readers place on actually finishing a novel that can move and comfort even its partial readers (and potentially, even those who haven't read a word).

Joyce's mythic method allows readers to read *Ulysses* in terms of the plot of the *Odyssey*, but a necessary consequence of his method is that the process also works in reverse. As the end of *Ulysses* approaches, it is clear that Joyce's novel is not going to end with Leopold Bloom slaughtering Blazes Boylan. Bloom's equanimity in "Ithaca" as he considers the possible list of Molly's suitors and Molly's psychological decision to choose Bloom at the end of "Penelope" foreground the nearly unremitting violence of the *Odyssey's* heroic ideology. Nowhere in *Ulysses* is a critical revision of the *Odyssey* clearer. Despite this revision of the violence of the Homeric heroic ideology, the *Odyssey* and *Ulysses* both use marriage and heterosexual romance as the testing ground that affirms the heroic qualities of the male protagonist—Odysseus can only return to his heroic identity when he passes Penelope's test of the bed, and Bloom defeats the suitors in Molly's memory of him.

The end of Lang's novel dispenses entirely with heroics and critiques the vision of human intimacy offered at the end of *Ulysses*. By rejecting heterosexual romance as a vehicle for narrative resolution, Lang uses *Ulysses* (and by extension, the *Odyssey*) to author a happy ending that affirms the power of authentic human connection and the freedom that might be gained from actually awaking from the nightmare of history. Stephen asks Nora—who will soon break up with Leo—to live in New York with him as platonic partners (he considers himself to be mostly asexual and has never been sexually attracted to her). Molly Bloom's "yes" hovers over the end of Lang's novel, which ultimately ends with a refusal. Nora reflects on Stephen's request and concludes that she "cannot say yes to Stephen":

> I can't say yes, she reflects. But how lucky I am that you don't need my yes. That you don't want my yes for the sake of a yes. You wouldn't believe it right now anyway. You'd roll your eyes if I said, "Yes! Let's do it. Let's go to New York and get the apartment". You'd say no. I could say yes, and you would say no. Because you know me. Because you've been with me this whole time.
>
> It's just like that night we leaned out the windows, except now we're on the ground. After everything that has happened, in the violet dark of night, I still lean into you beside me. And I know that you are there.
>
> (*SJ* 232)

The connection between Stephen and Nora makes it both impossible and unnecessary for her to say yes, to affirm him. This ending reads and revises the nostalgic impulse at the end of *Ulysses*. Lang's ending returns to the past, but it does not nostalgically remain there. Nora returns to the present and takes comfort in Stephen's continued presence for her. Lang's novel generates a quiet ecstasy by paying tribute to the bonds of friendship and celebrating the value of human intimacy that asks for nothing. The eighteenth chapter of *The Sixteenth of June* ends with an epiphanic presentation of an elusive, unbreakable bond of friendship.

But, *The Sixteenth of June* doesn't end there. The Afterword breaks free of the Joycean narrative structure completely to imagine its characters being released from the past into the future. Nora has left Leo and traveled to Milan after making peace with each of the Portmans. In the final moments of the novel, she thinks about the upcoming second anniversary of her mother's death but notes that her thoughts have been more preoccupied by her upcoming trip to Paris. This Afterword grants her the kind of peace (complete with a trip to Paris) that Stephen Dedalus sought when he pleaded with the ghost of his mother at the beginning of *Ulysses* to "let [him] be and let [him] live." The novel ends with her writing an email to Stephen: "*I don't know where it will all lead . . . But I'm glad . . . Even if it's all a little up in the air. For the first time in so long, I feel happy*" (*SJ* 237). The indeterminacy of Nora's life makes her happiness possible, and it makes a happy ending of Lang's novel possible—the narrative device here intersects with the character's experience. Nora pauses before she sends her email to reflect on her own words, as she "paused and examined them, testing them out . . . It looked right. She hit send" (*SJ* 237). The novel thus ends with an act of reading as self-reflection followed by an intimate communication that affirms her bond with Stephen.

In the afterword, *The Sixteenth of June* moves past the sixteenth of June and abandons its intertextual dialogue with *Ulysses* (which of course has no corresponding afterword) to depict this moment of happy self-reflection. The end of the novel manages to nearly forget the sixteenth of June in a way that revises the cultural meaning of commemorating it (and *Ulysses*). In Milan, Nora receives her invitation to the Portmans' Bloomsday party after the fact. In her new life in Italy, she nearly forgets Bloomsday, and recalls only when she is ordering gelato. She briefly thinks about the party she is missing and wonders about each of the members of the Portman family. This moment of Bloomsday commemoration has become radically personalized—the sixteenth of June becomes an occasion for Nora to recall her personal history as Lang's novel recalls its literary origins. Character and text confront the past, no longer a nightmare, and turn quietly toward an unknown, but promising future. If Odysseus's journey was at least in part motivated by his desire to rediscover and reclaim his identity as Odysseus, the King of Ithaca, then Lang's novel in its own way sends its twenty-first century characters on journeys of reading *Ulysses* in dynamic relation to their lives in order to author themselves and the terms by which they might be happy. The ancient, modern, and contemporary versions of the story of *Ulysses* self-consciously defend the critical value of the story as the medium through which the past is confronted and the future is made possible.

Going to the Mat for Joyce: *Fun Home* and the Future of Joyce's Classical Modernism

Alison Bechdel's 2006 graphic memoir *Fun Home* begins with a strikingly realistic drawing of Bechdel's father, Bruce, on the title page of the first chapter. He stands shirtless in the center of the frame, an arm bent, hand on his hip, with an expression on his face that betrays defiant dignity, vulnerability, and quiet suffering. He stares directly at Bechdel's reader. Beneath the frame is the title of the first chapter: "Old father, old artificer," a phrase that reaches back to Stephen Dedalus at the end of *Portrait* at the moment when he explicitly identifies his affiliation with both his mythic namesake and his son, Icarus. He mythologizes himself as father and son, creator and created. Bechdel's title page is a complex intertextual site that reaches back to Joyce reaching back to Ovid (reaching back to myth). In so doing, she reactivates Joyce's own model of classical reception as a vehicle for empathetic understanding and self-discovery as she attempts to come to terms with the complex intersection between her coming out and her father's suicide. Turning to Joyce offers Bechdel a mythic language to recount a history of sexual repression and trauma that might otherwise remain unspoken. Mythologizing her relationship to her father also grants Bechdel the analytic distance that she needs to tell this story. At times, she wryly engages with myth, seen when she describes her father's obsession with interior design and calls him a "Daedalus of décor."

Bechdel needed to turn to myth and to literature to tell her story, in large part because literature and myth provided the templates by which members of her family formed their identities. Excavating those identities required an elaborate reading process that moved fluidly between literature and lived experience. Ariela Freedman explains this process in the following way:

> The most tantalizing possibility that books offer is the possibly of self-invention. This Bechdel presents as a family pathology; in her hyper-artistic household, art is life. Her father is passionate about literature and understands himself through the paradigms presented both in works of fiction and in the autobiographies of writers like Fitzgerald—like Bechdel, he wants to read the life and work together as a single masterwork.[13]

Bruce and Bechdel are both drawn to writers such as Joyce, Wilde, Fitzgerald, and Camus in part because in different ways, they were literary celebrities whose works were and are read in terms of the canonized myths of their lives. The interpenetration of literature and lived experience shapes them as both biographically-oriented readers and as people viewing themselves and others as fiction. For a time, Bruce was Bechdel's high school English teacher; the experience of the classroom enabled an intellectual, aesthetic intimacy that was not possible in their family life. One panel shows the significance of this experience for them as they drive away from school, and Bruce tells his daughter, "You're the only one in that class worth teaching," to which she replies, "It's the only class I have worth taking" (*FH* 199).

By contrast, the college literature classroom has replaced the stifling classics classrooms of Joyce's fiction as spaces of institutional power against which the young writer must rebel in order to create. *Fun Home* interrogates some of the major assumptions underlying twentieth-century literary study by depicting the college classroom as a repressive, hegemonic, and limited site of reading. The modernist canon serves as a useful target for this interrogation because its consolidation in large part depended on reading practices that emerged in the era of New Criticism that privileged formal complexity and depersonalized reading practices. Bechdel's freshman English class would have taken place in the late 1970s, when critical theory was the dominant mode of academic literary analysis but also when the theory wars were already brewing about the value of theoretical approaches to literature. Above a frame depicting a bearded professor looming over his students, whose expressions range from boredom to intimidation to bemused interest, Bechdel notes that the experience of this class "confounded her." He asks them a question about Hemingway's *The Sun Also Rises* that is not atypical for a class entitled "Mythology and Archetypal Experience": "Do you see how Jake's renewal in Spain exactly follows the process of rebirth that Jung calls 'natural transformation'?" (*FH* 200). An embedded caption translates the mixture of irritation and confusion of Bechdel's expression: "I didn't understand why we couldn't just read the books without forcing contorted interpretations on them" (*FH* 200). Conrad's *Heart of Darkness* also becomes a site of conflict between the professor and his students. Above a frame depicting the professor angrily drawing on the board and saying, "Get it? Marlow's steamer? Penis. The Congo? Vagina," the caption reads, "Our teacher frequently grew exasperated with the whole class" (*FH* 200). This performance of reading is followed immediately by frames depicting Bechdel responding to her graded papers covered with her professor's rejection of her own writing ("ww" for "wrong word" being the most frequent comment, which leads Bechdel to ask, "is? How can 'is' be wrong?" [*FH* 201]). This juxtaposition reinforces the gatekeeping function of the English professor— Bechdel's substitute for Joyce's Latin teachers—who performs specialist readings and enforces the norms of academic expression on amateur writers. As *Fun Home* shows, the training of amateur students by the specialist reader begins with dispelling the student's inclination to view the literary text in terms of authorial intention—the first question a student asks of the professor's Jungian reading of *The Sun Also Rises* is, "You mean, like ... Hemingway did that on purpose?" (*FH* 200). The images accompanying these exchanges—the students' expressions of confusion, boredom, annoyance and the professor's expression of frustration—suggest an antagonistic relation between professional and amateur readers and modes of reading.

From the first frames, *Fun Home* presents Bruce Bechdel as an alternative to the professorial reader. He elaborates his reading of *The Sun Also Rises* to counter Bechdel's professor's Jungian reading: "It's a roman à clef, right? Jake is Hemingway. Cohn was a guy named Harold Loeb. Brett is Lady Duff Twysden" (*FH* 201). The memoir's third chapter shows him reading Fitzgerald's *This Side of Paradise* alongside Arthur Mizener's Fitzgerald biography, which suggests that he is drawn to modernist fiction precisely because it invites this kind of contextual reading. As Bechdel notes, "I think what was so alluring to my father about Fitzgerald's stories was their inextricability from Fitzgerald's life" (*FH* 65). Bechdel's reading of Joyce and Fitzgerald underscores the ways that their fiction depends on both their actual lived experience and the myths that were spun out of these experiences.

Because *Fun Home* is a graphic memoir, it would be nearly impossible to exclude the author from discussions of it. *Fun Home*'s characters and narrative praxis vitally depend on maintaining fluid boundaries between fiction and truth, art and life. The graphic memoir enables a wider interrogation of the ways one might read not only clearly autobiographical genres but also canonical literature. *Fun Home*'s presentation of Joyce best illustrates Bechdel's simultaneous disdain for canonical authority and eventual recognition of its potential power to inspire her own creativity. In an interview with Hilary Chute, Bechdel notes:

> I wrote all over that copy of *Ulysses*. It was sort of like fuck you. A fuck you both to my dad and to James Joyce because it was such an annoying book to read, really. I wrote in it as I was reading. Sometimes I would draw pictures over the page. I didn't want to treat the book reverentially.[14]

In a statement that echoes the words of Heaney, Walcott, McCann, and García Márquez, Bechdel identifies the process of reading Joyce—even in a hostile way—as the beginning of writing. The nature of her art as a cartoonist meant that her writing began as a palimpsest in the pages of *Ulysses*.

Critics have tended to read *Fun Home* as a challenge to the cultural authority of Joyce and high modernism in a medium usually not associated with high culture—they have argued that Bechdel is clearing a space for the graphic novel alongside the modernist novel in the literary canon. Although I mostly agree with this assessment, I would add that *Fun Home* also suggests that the graphic novel is actually the logical extension of the model of composition and reading evident in *Ulysses*, even though its antagonism toward institutional ways of reading Joyce is clear. As I have argued, Joyce's fiction presents readers who are able to identify with what they read (to a point) and who read as a form of self-discovery. Identification and invention are in fact the central operations of Bechdel's composition of *Fun Home* and readers' experience with the graphic form. The compositional history of *Fun Home* affirms the importance of identification to it. As Bechdel notes in an interview, she posed for all of the frames of *Fun Home* and used the photographs of herself (as herself, as her father, as Sylvia Beach, etc.) as the basis for all of the memoir's panels. By doing so, she grounded the very creation of *Fun Home* in a variety of acts of projection and identification. As she noted in an interview, "I had to be my dad, I had to be my mom, I had to be my parents fighting with one another ... and occasionally I would really get glimpses of what it must have felt like to be my father."[15] *Fun Home*'s composition therefore uniquely enables and mirrors its narrative depiction of Bechdel's attempts to identify with her father in order to make sense of their intertwined stories.

Fun Home's self-conscious reflections on reading train readers by exploiting the unique potential of the graphic medium for inviting readers to project themselves into the text. In his discussion of the universality of the simplified cartoon image, Scott McCloud notes that, "when you enter the world of the cartoon, you see yourself."[16] This narcissistic mode of seeing is of course not unique to comics—as Stephen Dedalus notes in the library, "We walk through ourselves, meeting robbers, ghosts, giants, old men, young men, wives, widows, brothers-in-love, but always meeting ourselves" (*U* 9.1044–6). However, comics have unique resources for amplifying this tendency. The more realistic and detailed a drawing of a person is, the more the viewer tends to view it as other. The relative simplicity of what Bechdel calls "the usual cartoony style" allows viewers to identify with the cartoon figure.[17] McCloud explains, "the cartoon is a vacuum into which our identity and awareness are pulled, an empty shell that we inhabit which enables us to travel in another realm. We don't just observe the cartoon, we become it."[18]

Comics invite readers toward a form of projection that intensifies Bruce Bechdel's reading praxis. Bechdel offers a mini-lesson in this kind of reading by describing her childhood affinity for *The Wind in the Willows*. She notes, "I took for granted the parallels between this landscape and my own. Our creek flowed in the same direction as Ratty's River" (*FH* 146). She concludes, "But the best thing about the *Wind in the Willows* map was its mystical bridging of the symbolic and the real, of the label and the thing itself. It was a chart, but also a vivid, almost animated picture. Look closely" (*FH* 147). The gentle final imperative transitions from Bechdel learning to read the cartoon image to her prompting her readers to a new kind of seeing, what McCloud calls closure, whereby the reader must be an active participant in the creation of the text's effects of time and motion.[19] Joyce's readers, who through the process of reading *Ulysses* have internalized maps of Dublin and tracked the movements of a throwaway on the Liffey according to the tides in June 1904, are deeply familiar with the kind of reading process that the cartoon requires because it overlaps in significant ways with the reading process *Ulysses* demands.

The reading process invited by *Fun Home* does more than just echo the reading process Joyce's fiction requires—the presence of Joyce's fiction within *Fun Home* suggests that Bruce and Bechdel learned this mode of reading from reading and misreading Joyce. *Fun Home* makes clear a divide between Bechdel's college-age self, who is the main character of her book, and the more mature author of the graphic memoir. *Fun Home* here aligns with *The Sixteenth of June*, because both works depend significantly on Joyce while featuring characters who can't stand reading his fiction. When Bechdel calls her father from college to tell him she is reading *A Portrait of the Artist as a Young Man*, he tells her, "Good. You damn well better identify with every page" (*FH* 201). She wants to identify with neither Joyce nor her father at that moment, so she does what she can to avoid literature classes altogether until she ends up being forced to take a winter session *Ulysses* course. The course description promises an "unhurried reading and examination of Joyce's *Ulysses*, open to anyone (especially freshmen and women) with an appetite for Joyce and a willingness to read, or re-read, *Dubliners* and *Portrait* prior to the first meeting" (*FH* 202). This description betrays the stated and unstated rules governing the *Ulysses* classroom—its professed interest in less experienced students and women, if anything, reinforces the usual demographics of the course as enthusiastic, experienced male readers. The actual course confirms this, as Bechdel is the only female student pictured in any of the frames representing the class—and the only one who is clearly not on board with the professor's way of reading. She listens with an expression of obvious displeasure as her professor and male peer construct the usual Homeric reading of *Ulysses* "much as the wise windbag, Nestor, might [have counseled] young Telemachus" (*FH* 206). A panel alongside this moment of male intellectual bonding reads, "Once you grasped that *Ulysses* was based on the *Odyssey*, was it really necessary to enumerate every last point of correspondence?" (*FH* 206). In this, she agrees with a significant line of Joyce critics who rejected this model of reading, including Ezra Pound, who in 1933 took this point further and argued in his distinctive way that, "the parallels with the *Odyssey* are mere mechanics, any blockhead can go back and trace them."[20] However, the next panel shows a perplexed Bechdel scowling at her copy of the novel in her dorm room and thinking, "what the fuck?" as she concedes, "without the Homeric clues, it certainly would be unreadable" (*FH* 207).

In the space of *Fun Home*, Bechdel the college student never finishes *Ulysses*. A frame shows her hand covering her closed eyes, her expression showing how excruciating the *Ulysses* class is to her as her professor and his Telemachus go through a reading of "Ithaca," which she has not read. The professor asks, "But even with the detailed scientific answers that this catechism provides, do we learn anything concrete about Bloom and Stephen's encounter? Do they connect?" over a frame that shows Bechdel's fountain pen drawing Bloom setting a candlestick on the floor over Joyce's "Ithaca" passage describing this gesture. Her mode of reading as she ignores the class discussion shows her taking ownership over the passage by visualizing it in her own medium, forging a personal and artistic connection to it even as she consciously rejects the discussion in which she remains silent. Years later, she answers the professor's question in the narrative of the next frame: "I had no idea. By the time the January term ended, I still had two hundred pages to go. And like Odysseus's men who had fallen in with the Lotus-Eaters, I felt no urgency to continue" (*FH* 209). Her academic experience with Joyce ends with her admission—I suspect shared by a reasonable number of students in the past century—that she "bullshat [her] way through the *Ulysses* exam" (*FH* 210).

But, this anticlimactic ending to her *Ulysses* course is not the end of her experience with Joyce, because *Fun Home* depends on an incredibly meticulous, creative, personal reading of *Ulysses*, especially the parts Bechdel never read in college. Her *Ulysses* course coincided with the moment in college when she was embarking on her process of coming out. Right after she had her pre-course interview with the *Ulysses* instructor, she goes to a bookstore where she realizes she is a lesbian while reading "Word is Out" as the Penguin Classics edition of *Odyssey* sits in the foreground of the frame. She relates this story via both Homer first and eventually via Joyce in relation to the classical tradition. She notes, "indeed, I embarked that day on an odyssey which, consisting as it did in a gradual, episodic, and inevitable convergence with my abstracted father, was very nearly as epic as the original" (*FH* 203). She notes her lack of patience for *Ulysses* when her own "odyssey was calling so seductively," setting up sexual, bodily pleasure and discovery as the urgent alternative to reading *Ulysses* (*FH* 207). She describes her process of reading *Lesbian Nation* and *Colette* as "one siren [leading] to another in an intertextual progression," thus identifying her process of sexual discovery as a reading process. She understands her terror of going to the "gay union" for the first time in Homeric terms: "Odysseus sailing to Hades could not have felt more trepidation than I did entering that room" (*FH* 210). Her rejection of Joyce within the narrative coincides with her creation of an alternate *Odyssey* of her own experience via a radically personalized mythic method.

But, *Fun Home's* major intertextual operations do not align with an Eliotic sense of a mythic method. *Portrait*, *Ulysses*, and the *Odyssey* exist as texts to be ignored, cast aside, read, misread, re-read, adapted, and totally remade by readers inside of *Fun Home's* plot, which depends on and depicts a high-stakes drama of searching for an enabling model of reading. *Fun Home's* narrative voice switches abruptly from a Homeric to a mixed Homeric-Joycean narrative after she comes out to her parents and learns that her father was closeted; the narrative remains in this mode until its ending. The transition occurs when Bechdel's father writes her a letter responding to her coming out and indirectly confesses his own history of repressed homosexual desire. Over a frame showing Bechdel reading this letter is a caption that adapts one of Joyce's questions from "Ithaca," part of *Ulysses* Bechdel's character had not yet read, a gap that reinforces the gap between the character's disdain and the author's dependence: "What, reduced to their simplest reciprocal form, were dad's thoughts about my thoughts about him, and his thoughts about my thoughts about his thoughts about me?" (*FH* 212). She continues to use Homeric characters to describe herself and her mother, but Joyce offers her the intertextual framework she needs to tell her father's story. During a drive to see "The Coal-Miner's Daughter," Bechdel depicts a moment of identification, when she learns that her father used to dress as a girl and reminds him that she dressed in boy's clothes. Joyce, not Homer, offers the literary prototype for this moment, as she notes, "It was not the sobbing, joyous reunion of Odysseus and Telemachus. It was more like fatherless Stephen and sonless Bloom having their equivocal late-night cocoa at 7 Eccles Street" (*FH* 221). She would only see her father once more before he died, but a caption on a page of the "Ithaca" episode of her copy of *Ulysses* reads, "We had had our Ithaca moment" (*FH* 222). *Ulysses* offers her an imaginative path toward resolving the end of her story with her father. Whereas a Homeric template would reinforce her failure to have a full resolution, *Ulysses* reassures her that the muted moment she shared with her father is common to the human experience at the level of everyday life. Bechdel depicts a page of her father's copy of *Ulysses*, the moment in "Hades" when Bloom is reminded of his father's suicide. To attempt to understand her father, she needs to read Joyce as he read and misread him.

Bechdel's final movements in *Fun Home* all depend on a textual, contextual, and biographical reading of Joyce and a reading of her father reading Joyce. She begins by drawing a letter he wrote to her mother when he courted her comparing her writing to Joyce's. He champions Joyce's line "and he asked me with his eyes" as "the best thing ever written—passion on paper who else could do it?" (*FH* 227). In the next frame, Bechdel draws the final page of *Ulysses*, without annotations that would indicate whether it was her copy or her father's, with a series of embedded captions that move from her father's misreading to the contextual reading she needs to understand him. She points out that her father made a "telling mistake … [imputing] the beseeching eyes to Bloom instead of to his wife, Molly," and she highlights the correct line on the page pictured in the frame (*FH* 228). This misreading helps her to ask the memoir's crucial question: "But how could he admire Joyce's lengthy, libidinal 'yes' so fervently and end up saying 'no' to his own life?" (*FH* 228). Her own reading offers her the answer: "I suppose that a lifetime spent hiding one's erotic truth could have a cumulative renunciatory effect. Sexual shame is in itself a kind of death" (*FH* 228). In a way that echoes Bloom and Molly sharing the memory of "met him pike hoses," Bechdel came to understand Bruce by reconstructing his misreadings.

Retracing Bruce's reading of *Ulysses* enabled Bechdel to discover the kind of urgency of Joyce's fiction that seemed to have no place in her stifling college classroom. She recounts Joyce's history of censorship in the final pages on the novel and notes that she likes to think that Margaret Anderson and Jane Heap, the editors of the *Little Review*, and Sylvia Beach and Adrienne Monnier, the publishers of *Ulysses*, "went to the mat for this book because they were lesbians, because they knew a thing or two about erotic truth" (*FH* 229). As she tells this story, she draws the iconic photograph of Joyce and Beach leaning against the doorway of Beach's famous Parisian bookstore Shakespeare and Company. Recalling Bechdel's compositional process, this drawing conveys that she actually posed as both Joyce and Beach before she drew this picture. Bechdel ultimately reads Joyce in order to discover herself, her father, and Joyce inside of her own book.

This reading enables her to write a different ending for herself and her father. The book's final frames depict her father standing in a pool, looking up at her as she stands on a diving board, preparing to jump to him. The caption returns to Joyce's "theme that spiritual, not consubstantial, paternity is the important thing" and asks, "is it so unusual for the two things to coincide?" (*FH* 231). She continues, "What if Icarus hadn't hurtled into the sea? What if he'd inherited his father's inventive bent? What might he have wrought?" (*FH* 231). Joyce's model of historical imagination offers her a way to craft the personal mythological image she has searched for from *Fun Home*'s opening frames. Stephen's artistic future was made possible by his serious imaginative engagement with a version of history and of reality that embraces the "actuality of the possible as possible" (*U* 2.67). In Chapter 2, I argued that this mode of historical imagination is not escapism for Stephen—rather, it grants him an alternative to violent, teleological models of the future. Bechdel's turn to possibility here is also not escapism—the very next frame pictures the front of the truck that killed her father, thereby identifying with him in the most painful, terrifying moment of his life, along with the caption, "He did hurtle into the sea, of course" (*FH* 232). The final frame depicts Bechdel as a child in mid-air, leaping to her father, who is ready to catch her. The caption reads, "But in the tricky reverse narration that impels out entwined stories, he was there to catch me when I leapt" (*FH* 232). Reactivating Joyce's mode of classical reading generates a personal mythology that can emerge from these entwined stories without surrendering to erotic shame, silence, despair, or death. Bechdel's engagement with Joyce underscores the personal urgency of this kind of work for Joyce, those who published him, those who read him, and those who re-write him. Bechdel's work reminds us of the personal risks Joyce took to offer his particular contribution to the classical tradition. Both authors envision the classical world as an ally to personal, aesthetic, psychological, social, political, and sexual freedom.

When we examine twenty-first century classical receptions in a global context, we discover that in many cases the classics in question have traveled through Ireland and been reimagined by Joyce. His idiosyncratic, energetic readings of different lines of classical transmission—including translations in multiple languages; some original Greek and Latin texts; at least a century of classical criticism; and contemporary and earlier adaptations by other artists working in various media—remind us that classical reception has perhaps never been an unmediated exchange between the modern and ancient artist. Joyce looms in contemporary literature, not because of his academic prestige and cultural capital. He has emboldened some of the best-known contemporary writers to take artistic risks because of the high stakes he understood to be central to the modern literary enterprise. His imaginative, rebellious classical vision offers an important alternative lineage to the most limited, parochial versions of Classics as a discipline that have come under attack in the culture wars of the past several decades (some coming from within the discipline of Classics itself). With the decline of Classics departments across the twentieth century, Joyce emerged as a new classic embodying a logic of cultural prestige his works refused. The writings of Bechdel, Lang, McBride, Walcott, Heaney, García Márquez, McCann, and others, such as Edna O'Brien and Samuel Beckett, remind us of how little Joyce's writing has in common with the institutions that have championed his work. As I discussed at the outset of this study, both classical and modernist studies scholars have been expanding the boundaries of their disciplines to argue for a more urgent relevance of their fields to contemporary life. Joyce shared this sense of struggle and is an important forerunner to these conversations. His work's insistence that human beings and societies are always open to revision and change and that the act of reading can initiate personal and cultural transformation has perhaps never been more important.

Richard Ellmann opens his monumental biography of Joyce by writing, "We are still learning to be James Joyce's contemporaries, to understand our interpreter" (*JJ* 3).[21] Bechdel's work exposes the limitations of a canonical reading grounded in a notion of an idealized later reading process that can be free of shortcomings. Her work follows Joyce's in its skepticism of canons and the notion of later, better readings. However, her work also shares with Joyce's a sense of hope about later, better readers. Joyce's epic knew that historical change would not be mandated by the gods and that history was not, as Mr. Deasy suspected, moving "towards one great goal, the manifestation of God" (*U* 2.380–1). In response to this, Stephen listened to the voices of the boys playing in the school yard, "jerked his thumb" towards the window, and said, "That is God ... A shout in the street" (*U* 2.382–6). In response to a teleological historical argument, Stephen instinctively pointed to children as the drivers of what would happen next, even though readers in 1922 knew that many of them would die in the violent catastrophes of the First World War and the Irish struggle for independence and Civil War. In so doing, *Ulysses* addresses the present in terms of potential for the immediate future by inviting readers into the text as a space of potential transformation. As the novel suggests, human identity is open to rewriting and need not be confined by nightmares of history or by narrow ideas about the future. By inviting its readers to participate in the act of creating meaning, Joyce's fiction invites them to become authors of themselves and of alternate futures. As Bechdel, Lang, McBride, Heaney, McCann, García Márquez, and Walcott demonstrate, Joyce's fiction denies its readers a sense of epistemological mastery and demands that they ask, again and again, what comes next.

Notes

Introduction: Reading and Reception in Joyce's Classical Modernism

1 Joyce, *A Portrait of the Artist as a Young Man*, *The Egoist* (February 2, 1914), 50.

2 As Fritz Senn argues, Joyce's use of Latin in the epigraph of *Portrait* reactivates an ancient model of reading conditioned by Latin's word endings and flexible word order. Noting the intersection between the ancient and modern elements of Joyce's work, he observes, "So, for all his extravagant modernity, Joyce also turned back to reinstate an ancient technique to spell out meanings by sending the mind forward and backward." Senn, "The Challenge: 'Ignotas Animum' (An Old-Fashioned Close-Guessing at a Borrowed Structure)," *James Joyce Quarterly* 16, no. 1–2 (Fall 1978-Winter 1979), 123–34.

3 David Spurr offers an important evaluation of Kiberd's use of terms such as "real people" and "ordinary citizen." See David Spurr, "How to Read *Ulysses*," Review of Declan Kiberd, Ulysses *and Us*, 2009. James Joyce Broadsheet 84 (October 2009), 1.

4 Kiberd, Ulysses *and Us: The Art of Everyday Life in Joyce's Masterpiece* (New York: Norton, 2009), 16.

5 Jennifer Howard, "Status of the Humanities: We Haven't Quite Recovered from the Recession," *The Chronicle of Higher Education* (June 19, 2014). Web. Accessed October 9, 2018. If any future scholar of this period wants to know where to start in understanding what happened to the study of the humanities, she might consider reading Eric Hayot's piece whose title perfectly sums up the zeitgeist of the past decade: "The Sky Is Falling." *Profession*, Humanities Commons, Modern Languages Association (May 21, 2018). Web. Accessed October 15, 2018.

6 Mao and Walkowitz, "The New Modernist Studies," *PMLA* 123, no. 3 (May 2008): 737–48.

7 Lorna Hardwick, *Reception Studies* (Oxford: Oxford University Press, 2003), 2.

8 Ibid., 4.

9 Hardwick and Stray, *A Companion to Classical Receptions* (Oxford: Blackwell, 2008), 3.

10 Hickman, Introduction, *The Classics in Modernist Translation* (London: Bloomsbury, 2019), 2.

11 This point of view owes much to Sean Latham's *Am I a Snob? Modernism and the Novel* (Ithaca: Cornell University Press, 2003).

12 R.J. Schork, *Latin and Roman Culture in Joyce* (Gainesville: University Press of Florida, 1997), 10.

13 Seth Schein, "'Our Debt to Greece and Rome': Canon, Class, and Ideology," In Hardwick and Stray, eds., *A Companion to Classical Receptions*, 78.

14 See, Gregory Dobbins, *Lazy Idle Schemers: Irish Modernism and the Cultural Politics of Idleness* (Dublin: Field Day Publications, 2010), especially the introduction, 1–31; Emer Nolan, "Modernism and the Irish Revival," in Joe Cleary and Claire Connolly, eds., *The Cambridge Companion to Modern Irish Culture* (Cambridge: Cambridge University Press, 2005), 157–72.

15 A. Nicholas Fargnoli and Michael Patrick Gillespie, *A Critical Companion to James Joyce* (New York: Facts on File, 2006), 318–19.

16 Chris Baldick, *The Oxford Dictionary of Literary Terms*, 3rd edition. 2008. Online version accessed 10 May 2018.

17 Michael Levenson, "Modernisms," in John McCourt, ed., *James Joyce in Context* (Cambridge: Cambridge University Press, 2009), 270.

18 Also quoted in Christopher Butler, "Joyce, the Modernist," in Derek Attridge, *Cambridge Companion to James Joyce* (Cambridge: Cambridge University Press, 2004), 69.

19 The best study I have seen on the vexed history of "modernism" as an idea is Sean Latham and Gayle Rogers, *Modernism: The Evolution of an Idea* (Bloomsbury: Bloomsbury Press, 2015).

20 Richard Aldington, "Le Latin Mystique," *The Egoist* (March 16, 1914).

21 Aldington, "Anti-Hellenism: A Note on Some Modern Art," *The Egoist* 2, no. 1 (January 15, 1914), 36.

22 I have written elsewhere about the significance of censorship to Joyce's writing in "'Cyclops,' Censorship, and Joyce's Monster Audiences," *James Joyce Quarterly* 48, no. 3 (Spring 2011): 425–44. That article and this book are indebted to the work of John Nash (*James Joyce and the Act of Reception*), Katherine Mullin (*James Joyce, Sexuality, and Social Purity*), Michael Groden, Celia Marshik (*British Modernism and Censorship*), and Paul Vanderham (*James Joyce and Censorship*).

23 Diego Angeli, "An Italian Comment on Portrait," trans. Joyce, *The Egoist* 5, no. 2 (February 1918): 30. Also in Robert H. Deming, *James Joyce: The Critical Heritage* (Delhi: Vikas Publishers, 1970), 116.

24 "Aramis," "The Scandal of *Ulysses*," *Sporting Times*, No. 34 (1 April 1922), 4. Also in Robert H. Deming, *James Joyce: The Critical Heritage, vol. 1 (1902–1927)*, 193.

25 Aldington, "The Influence of Mr. James Joyce," *English Review* 32 (April 1921),

333–41. Qtd in Charles Doyle, *Richard Aldington: A Biography* (Carbondale: Southern Illinois University, 1989), 94.

26 Eliot, "*Ulysses*, Order, and Myth," *Selected Prose of T.S. Eliot*, ed. Frank Kermode (London: Faber, 1975), 177. See Flack, *Modernism and Homer* (Cambridge: Cambridge University Press, 2015), 7–8; and Kevin Dettmar, *The Illicit Joyce of Postmodernism: Reading Against the Grain* (Madison: University of Wisconsin Press, 1996), 162–8.

27 Charles Doyle, *Richard Aldington: A Biography*, 94.

28 Erich Auerbach, *Mimesis: The Representation of Reality in Western Literature* (Princeton: Princeton University Press, 1968), 23.

29 John Pentland Mahaffy, *Social Life in Greece: From Homer to Menander* (London: Macmillan, 1877), 1.

30 Wilde argued that the *Iliad* presents "the pathetic side of woman's nature," but the *Odyssey* offers a view of "woman's nature and all its complexity and infinite variety of love and passion, of grief and joy, of desire and purity." *The Women of Homer* (London: The Oscar Wilde Society, 2008), 47.

31 In a different vein, see John Nash's *James Joyce and the Act of Reception*, which argues that "Joyce's work rewrites the responses of several actual readers and, in doing so, engages with the specific conditions of reception, notably in Ireland" (2).

32 Hugh Kenner, "On the Centenary of James Joyce." *New York Times*. January 31, 1982. www.nytimes.com/books/00/01/09/specials/joyce-centenary.html. Accessed October 28, 2016. See also Mary Power, "The Discovery of Ruby." *James Joyce Quarterly* 18.2 (Winter 1981): 115–21.

33 Stuart Gilbert, *James Joyce's* Ulysses (New York: Vintage, 1955), 41–2.

34 Ibid., 34.

35 Leo Bersani, "Against *Ulysses*," in *James Joyce's* Ulysses*: A Casebook*, ed. Derek Attridge (Oxford: Oxford University Press, 2004), p. 224.

36 Leonard Diepeeven, *The Difficulties of Modernism* (New York: Routledge, 2003), p 134.

37 Kiberd, *Ulysses and Us*, p. 8.

38 As Kenner points out, the source of this error is not, as Bloom presumes, Molly, but rather Bloom himself—Molly never pronounces the word in "Calypso." Kenner, *Ulysses* (Baltimore: Johns Hopkins University Press, 1987), 82.

39 Hickman, *The Classics in Modernist Translation*, 3.

40 Theodore Ziolkowski, *Classicism of the Twenties* (Chicago: University of Chicago Press 2015), 7.

41 T.E. Hulme, *Speculations: Essays on Humanism and the Philosophy of Art*, ed. Hubert Read (London: Routledge, 1960), 133. Ezra Pound, *Literary Essays*, ed. T.S. Eliot (New York: New Directions, 1935), 3.

42 Pound, *Selected Letters 1907–1941*, ed. D.D. Paige (New York: New Directions, 1950), 11.

43 Bradley, Bruce, S.J. "At School Together in Conmee's Time: Some Notes on Joyce's Clongowes Jesuit," *Dublin James Joyce Journal*, Number 3 (2010): 1–18. Also see W.B. Stanford, *Ireland and the Classical Tradition* (Dublin: Allen Figgis, 1976), 22.

44 William Corcoran, S.J., *Studies in the History of Classical Teaching* (New York: Benzinger Brothers, 1911), xiv and xviii.

45 W.B. Stanford, *Ireland and the Classical Tradition*, 34.

46 Schork, *Latin and Roman Culture in Joyce*, Chapter 2.

47 See Christopher Stray, *Classics Transformed: Schools, Universities, and Society in England 1830–1960* (Oxford: Clarendon Press, 1998).

48 On this scene and its cultural meanings, see Schork, *Greek Culture in Joyce*, 28–9 and Chapter 2.

49 On this, see Joseph Farrell, "Joyce and Modernist Latinity," in William Brickliss, et al., eds., *Reception and the Classics* (Cambridge: Cambridge University Press, 2012), 57–72.

50 Francoise Waquet, *Latin, Empire of the Sign from the Sixteenth to the Twentieth Century*, trans. John Howe (London: Verso, 2001), 83.

51 Ibid.

52 As Kevin Dettmar points out, Stuart Gilbert's exposition of Eliot's mythical method in his study of *Ulysses* deploys the novel's structure to respond to charges of the book's formlessness and also its vulgarity. Gilbert identifies himself as a member of those "who admired *Ulysses* for its structural, enduring qualities and not for the occasional presence in it of words and descriptive passages which shocked our elders." Quoted in Kevin Dettmar, "'Working in Accord with Obstacles': A Postmodern Perspective on Joyce's 'Mythical Method,'" in Dettmar, ed., *Re-reading the New: A Backward Glance at Modernism* (Ann Arbor: University of Michigan Press, 1992), 283.

53 There has been a recent critical turn toward evaluating the legacies of Joyce and modernism. For example, see Martha Carpentier, ed. *Joycean Legacies* (London: Palgrave Macmillan, 2015); Paige Reynolds, *Modernist Afterlives in Irish Literature and Culture* (London: Anthem Press, 2016); David James, ed. *The Legacies of Modernism: Historicising Postwar and Contemporary Fiction* (Cambridge: Cambridge University Press, 2011); David James, *Modernist Futures: Innovation and Inheritance in the Contemporary Novel* (Cambridge: Cambridge University Press, 2012).

54 Nola Tully, ed. *Yes I Said Yes I Will Yes: A Celebration of James Joyce, Ulysses, and 100 Years of Bloomsday* (New York: Vintage Books, 2004), 77.

1. Joyce's Classical Passwords

1   J.F. Byrne. *Silent Years: An Autobiography with Memoirs of James Joyce and Our Ireland* (New York: Farrar, Straus & Young, 1953), 23.

2   Bruce Bradley, S.J., *James Joyce's Schooldays* (New York: St. Martin's Press, 1982), 113.

3   Byrne, *Silent Years*, 264.

4   Ibid., 265.

5   Ibid., 264.

6   Eliot, "*Ulysses*, Order, and Myth," *Selected Prose of T.S. Eliot*, ed. Frank Kermode (London: Faber, 1975), 177.

7   Byrne, *Silent Years*, 264.

8   James Joyce Papers, Harry Ransom Center, Box 6, Folder 7, notebook 2.

9   W.B. Ready, "Review of *Silent Years*," *America* (May 15, 1954). James Joyce Papers, Harry Ransom Center, Box 7, folder 9.

10 James Boswell, *The Life of Samuel Johnson, Vol. 2* (New York: Harper, 1859), 250. I thank Stephanie Nelson for helping me to contextualize this history and for pointing me to this example.

11 Kenneth Haynes, "Gentleman's Latin, Lady's Greek," *The Oxford Companion to the Victorian Novel*, ed. Lisa Rodensky (Oxford: Oxford University Press, 2013), 418. But he also argues that it is a good deal more complex than this: ". . . classical allusions, far from expressing simple solidarity among gentlemen (who did not constitute a unified group) were used to distinguish competing claimants to gentlemanly status as well as introduce new ones" (419).

12 See Francoise Waquet, *Latin, or The Empire of the Sign: From the Sixteenth to the Twentieth Centuries* (London: Verso, 2002), 215. Also see 207–29.

13 As Colin MacCabe argues, "Modernism can be read as attempts to make up for the inadequacies of audiences in the present by postulating ideal audiences in the future." MacCabe, *On the Eloquence of the Vulgar: Language, Cinema, and the Politics of Culture* (London: Bloomsbury Press, 1999), 11. Nash disagrees and argues that, "Joyce's writing is addressed to the very question of an audience or a public, especially as constituted in Ireland in the period of his work." *James Joyce and the Act of Reception: Reading, Ireland, Modernism* (Cambridge: Cambridge University Press, 2006), 7.

14 Robert Scholes and Richard Kain, eds. *The Workshop of Dedalus* (Evanston: Northwestern University Press, 1965), 142.

15 Ibid.

16 Schork, *Latin and Roman Culture in Joyce*, 3.

17 M.M. Bakhtin, *The Dialogic Imagination*, ed. Michael Holquist, trans. Caryl Emerson and Michael Holquist (Austin: University of Texas Press, 1982), 23.

18 Vicki Mahaffey and Michael Groden, "Silence and Fractals in 'The Sisters,'" in
   Collaborative Dubliners: Joyce in Dialogue, ed. Mahaffey (Syracuse: Syracuse
   University Press, 2012), 36.

19 As Saikat Majumdar observes, "the boys' world in *Dubliners* is one where the
   lowbrow exotica of the Apache Chief in boys' magazines such as *The Halfpenny
   Marvel* is held in ironic contrast to Julius Caesar's *Gallic Wars." Prose of the World:
   Modernism and the Banality of Empire* (Columbia: Columbia University Press,
   2013), 47.

20 See, for example, Sean P. Murphy, *James Joyce and Victims: Reading the Logic of
   Exclusion* (Fairleigh Dickinson University Press, 2003), 45–6.

21 Backus and Valente, "'An Encounter': James Joyce's Humiliation Nation," in
   Collaborative Dubliners: Joyce in Dialogue, ed. Vicki Mahaffey (Syracuse: Syracuse
   University Press, 2012), 36.

22 Backus and Valente, "'An Encounter: Joyce's Humiliation Nation," 62.

23 Margot Norris quotes Sedgwick in *Suspicious Reading of Joyce's* Dubliners
   (Philadelphia: University of Pennsylvania Press, 2003), 37.

24 My reading of Wilde's influence on Joyce owes much to chapters by Margot Norris
   ("A Walk on the Wild(e) Side: the Doubled Reading of 'An Encounter'"), Jean-
   Michel Rabaté ("On Joycean and Wildean Sodomy"), and Joseph Valente
   ("'Thrilled by his touch': the Aestheticizing of Homosexual Panic in *A Portrait of
   the Artist as a Young Man*") in *Quare Joyce*, ed. Valente (Ann Arbor: University of
   Michigan Press, 1998), 19–76.

25 Norris, *Suspicious Readings*, 44.

26 See Richard Brown, *James Joyce and Sexuality* (Cambridge: Cambridge University
   Press, 1985), 103.

27 See Karen Lawrence, *The Odyssey of Style in* Ulysses (Princeton: Princeton
   University Press, 1981), 83–90.

28 The main English *Odyssey* Joyce consulted, the Butcher and Lang translation reads,
   "On the one side there are beetling rocks, and against them the great wave roars of
   dark-eyed Amphitrite. These, ye must know, are they the blessed gods call the
   Rocks Wandering." *The* Odyssey *of Homer*, trans. S.H. Butcher and Andrew Lang
   (New York: Macmillan, 1906), 94.

29 In this, I agree with Michael Rubenstein, who writes in another context that the
   episode signals Joyce's particular brand of difficult modernism. The difficulty of
   "Wandering Rocks" emerges not "in the service of a modernist difficulty-for-its-
   own-sake but rather in the service of a mimetic modernism trying to outdo—not,
   crucially, undo—narrative realism." "City Circuits: 'Aeolus' and 'Wandering Rocks,'"
   in *The Cambridge Companion to* Ulysses, ed. Sean Latham (Cambridge:
   Cambridge University Press, 2014), 113.

30 Trevor Williams, "Conmeeism and the Universe of Discourse in 'Wandering Rocks,'" *James Joyce Quarterly* 29, no. 2 (Winter, 1992), 270.

31 As Vincent Cheng points out, Bloom sees the sign advertising Conmee's sermon and offers a perspective on missionary work in a way that complicates and critiques Conmee's logic of White Man's Burden. *Joyce, Race, and Empire* (Cambridge: Cambridge University Press, 1995), 179.

32 Stuart Gilbert, *James Joyce's Ulysses* (New York: Vintage, 1955), 239.

33 Platt, *Joyce and the Anglo-Irish: A Study of Joyce and the Literary Revival* (Amsterdam: Rodopi, 1998), 93.

34 Norris, *Virgin and Veteran Readings of Ulysses* (New York: Palgrave, 2011), 73–4.

35 Williams argues that the mental shift into Latin protects Conmee, offering him a shield from sexually graphic language he is too embarrassed to think in English. Williams, "Conmeeism," 275.

36 See Phillip Lawton, "For the gentleman and the scholar: Sexual and Scatological References in the Loeb Classical Library," in *Expurgating the Classics: Editing Out in Greek or Latin*, eds. Steven Harrison and Christopher Stray (London: Bloomsbury Academic Press, 2012). Available from: eBook Academic Collection (EBSCOhost), Ipswich, MA. Accessed June 9, 2017.

37 Brown, *James Joyce and Sexuality*, 58. For Brown's thorough background on Joyce's reading of Paul Garnier's *Onanisme* and his interest in medical and Catholic distinctions of sex (including his notes on this Latin phrase for *Exiles*), see 54–62. Norris argues that Conmee's speculation is an attempt to titillate by imaginatively trying to pry into Mary Rochfort's secrets. *Virgin and Veteran Readings*, 72.

38 Later, when Ezra Pound objected to the manuscript of "Sirens" on the grounds that it once again illustrated Joyce's "obsessions arseore-ial, cloacal, deist, aesthetic," Joyce defended this dimension of his fiction by concluding that the grounds of Pound's disapproval were "not legitimate." *Pound/Joyce,* ed. Forrest Read, 158–60.

39 Unsigned review, *Everyman*, 23 February 1917, in Deming, *James Joyce: The Critical Heritage,* Vol. 1, 398. Especially relevant here is Michael Rubenstein's excellent work exposing the crucial role of public utilities in Joyce's depiction of Irish life specifically and in Irish modernism more generally. See *Public Works: Infrastructure, Irish Modernism, and the Postcolonial* (South Bend: University of Notre Dame Press, 2010).

40 Valente, "'Thrilled by His Touch': The Aestheticizing of Homosexual Panic in *A Portrait of the Artist as a Young Man*," in *Quare Joyce*, ed. Valente (Ann Arbor: University of Michigan Press, 2000), 53–5.

41 Valente, "'Thrilled by His Touch,'" 54.

42 J.J. Atherton has identified the textbook as *Kennedy's Latin Primer* in his edition of *Portrait* (London: Heinemann, 1964). On this, see Schork, *Latin and Roman*

Culture in Joyce, 49; and R. Brandon Kershner, *Joyce, Bakhtin, and Popular Culture: Chronicles of Disorder* (Chapel Hill: University of North Carolina Press, 1989), 216–17.

43 I discuss this statue in more detail in Chapter 3. On this history, see Christine Havelock, *The Aphrodite of Knidos and Her Successors: A Historical Review of the Female Nude in Greek Art* (Ann Arbor: University of Michigan Press, 2007), 10–13; and Valerie Bénéjam, "Stephen and the Venus of Praxiteles: The Backside of Aesthetics," in *Cultural Studies in James Joyce*, ed. R.B. Kershner (Amsterdam: Rodopi, 2003), 59–76.

44 Bernard Benstock argues that this drawing is "the obvious parody of female genitalia." Although I do not share the sense that this implication is obvious, I think it is certainly possible. I also think it is a point of indeterminacy, which heightens the illicit nature of the scene. See Benstock, "Inscribing James Joyce's Tombstone," in *Coping with Joyce: Essays from the Copenhagen Symposium*, Morris Beja and Shari Benstock, eds. (Columbus: The Ohio State University Press, 1989), 86. I thank Claire Culleton for pointing this out to me.

45 Building on Spivak's notion of "alienated assent" in "The Burden of English," Gregory Castle notes, ". . . while [denominational schools] offered a superior grade of education, they also exposed students to forms of eroticized pedagogical violence perhaps unique to colonial education." *Reading the Modernist Bildungsroman* (Gainesville: University Press of Florida, 2006), 164.

46 See Ellmann, *James Joyce*, 289 for a description of Hugh MacNeill, the person from whom Joyce formed this character.

47 Schork, *Latin and Roman Culture in Joyce*, 217.

48 Eugene Sheehy, *The Joyce We Knew*, ed. Ulick O'Connor (Cork: Mercier Press, 1967), 22. Also qtd. in Schork, *Latin and Roman Culture in Joyce*, 217.

49 Stanislaus Joyce, *My Brother's Keeper: James Joyce's Early Years* (Cambridge, MA: DeCapo Press, 1958), 211–12. The phrasing of this statement in Stanislaus's book creates ambiguity about whether Byrne or Cosgrave said it. A letter from Ellmann in Byrne's archive at the Harry Ransom Center clarifies that it was Byrne. Letter dated November 3, 1955, James Joyce Papers, Harry Ransom Center, Box 5, folder 5.

50 Marc Mamigonian and Joel Turner, "Annotations to *Stephen Hero*," *James Joyce Quarterly* 40, no. 3 (Spring, 2003): 412.

51 Schork, *Latin and Roman Culture in Joyce*, 220.

52 Ibid.

53 Deming, Robert H. *James Joyce. Volume I: 1907–27*. London: Routledge, 1997. EBSCOhost.

54 The opening of the 1904 edition reads: "Three nights in succession I had found myself in Great Britain-street at that hour, as if by Providence. Three nights also I

had raised my eyes to that lighted square of window and speculated. I seemed to understand it would occur at night. But in spite of the Providence that had led my feet, and in spite of the reverent curiosity of my eyes, I had discovered nothing. Each night the square was lighted in the same way, faintly and evenly. It was not the light of candles, so far as I could see. Therefore, it had not yet occurred."

55 Recently Claire Culleton and Ellen Scheible have convincingly called for a new reading of *Dubliners*, one that moves away from characterizing Dublin in terms of paralysis, an intellectual move that reproduces colonialist logics. See *Rethinking Joyce's* Dubliners (New York: Palgrave, 2017).

56 Kevin Sullivan, *Joyce Among the Jesuits* (New York: Columbia University Press, 1958), 41.

57 Groden and Mahaffey, "Silence and Fractals in 'The Sisters,'" in *Collaborative Dubliners: Joyce in Dialogue*, ed. Vicki Mahaffey (Syracuse: Syracuse University Press, 2012), 30.

58 Ibid., 31.

59 Senn, "Gnomon Inverted," in *ReJoycing: New Readings of* Dubliners, eds. Rosa M. Bollitieri Bosinelli and Harold F. Mosher (Louisville: University Press of Kentucky, 1998), 250.

60 Senn, "Gnomon Inverted," 256.

61 Murray McArthur, "'The Index Nothing Affirmeth': The Semiotic Formation of a Literary Mandate in Joyce's 'The Sisters,'" *James Joyce Quarterly* 45, no. 2 (Winter, 2008): 250.

62 Schork, *Greek and Hellenic Culture in Joyce*, 87. "Odysseus" etymologically suggests both "one who suffers" and "one who causes suffering," or as George Dimock puts it, "Trouble." The Butcher and Lang translation Joyce read translates Odysseus's name as "a man of wrath" (323). For a full discussion of Odysseus's name, see Dimock, "The Name of Odysseus" *Hudson Review* 9, no. 1 (Spring 1956): 54–7.

2. "So Let the Ruins Rot": Joyce and Historical Apathy

1 In a similar vein, on September 25, 1906, Joyce wrote to Stanislaus about his visit to the Forum and his response to the throngs of tourists occupying that site. He concluded, "Rome reminds me of a man who lives by exhibiting to travelers his grandmother's corpse" (Letters II 165). Also see Spoo, *James Joyce and the Language of History*, 15.

2 Robert Spoo, *James Joyce and the Language of History* (Oxford: Oxford University Press, 1994), 8.

3 Andrew Gibson, *Joyce's Revenge: History, Politics, and Aesthetics in* Ulysses (Oxford: Oxford University Press, 2002), 22–3.

4 Len Platt, *Joyce and the Anglo-Irish: A Study of Joyce and the Literary Revival* (Amsterdam: Rodopi, 1998), 8.

5 Gibson, *Joyce's Revenge*, 113.

6 Ibid., 17.

7 On display here is what Michael Patrick Gillespie has evaluated as Joyce's rancor, as a key modality in his construction of exile in his fiction. See *James Joyce and the Exilic Imagination* (Gainesville: University of Florida Press, 2015), 15 and *passim*.

8 Ibid., 114.

9 Clare Hutton offers a useful history of revivalism that helps to contextualize the arguments against what she calls the deficiencies of revivalist ideology. See "Joyce and the Institutions of Revivalism," *Irish University Review* 33, no. 1 (Spring–Summer 2003): 117–32. For a more general consideration of the relationship between the Revival and modernism in Ireland, see Rónán McDonald, "The Irish Revival and Modernism," in *The Cambridge Companion to Irish Modernism* (Cambridge: Cambridge University Press, 2014): 51–62.

10 Kevin Sullivan, *Joyce Among the Jesuits* (New York: Columbia University Press, 1958), 237.

11 See R.J. Schork, *Latin and Roman Culture in Joyce*, 40–75.

12 Ibid., 159.

13 Joe Dillon, "The Classics at the Wake: Some Aspects of Classical Influence in Joyce's *Finnegans Wake*," *Classics Ireland*, vol. 5 (1998): 9–29. See 10–13 for a more detailed description of Joyce's education.

14 Murnaghan and Roberts, *Childhood and the Classics, Britain and America 1850–1965* (Oxford: Oxford University Press, 2018), 136.

15 Ibid., 139. Joyce's readers will recognize that this precisely describes the formation of Stephen Dedalus in *Portrait* and what Fritz Senn identifies as an important historiographic insight of *Ulysses*: "History is not alone what happens to have been preserved, but in particular what we are able to know, what we can assimilate, what fits into our world views, our mental capacity. History is what has been related to us and what we can relate to." Senn, "History as Text in Reverse," *James Joyce Quarterly*, vol. 28, no. 4 (Summer 1991): 770.

16 Bruce Bradley, S.J. *James Joyce's Schooldays* (New York: St. Martin's Press, 1982), 42–43. Joyce used this in *Portrait*, but changed the groups to York and Lancaster, presumably to intensify the scene's colonial dimensions.

17 Stanislaus Joyce, *My Brother's Keeper*, 46.

18 For example, Jim Norton's audio recording uses the same voice for Dante and for these lines, which is one possibility.

19 Robert E. Scholes and Richard Morgan Kain, eds. *The Workshop of Dedalus: James Joyce and the Raw Materials for* A Portrait of the Artist as a Young Man (Evanston: Northwestern University Press, 1965), 11.

20 See Spoo, *James Joyce and the Language of History*, 45–7 and R. Brandon Kershner, *Joyce, Bakhtin, and Popular Culture: Chronicles of Disorder* (Chapel Hill: University of North Carolina Press, 1989), 216–21.

21 John Simpson, "Peter Parley's Tales of the Ancients," *James Joyce Online Notes.* www.jjon.org/joyce-s-allusions/peter-parley.

22 Samuel Griswold Goodrich, *Tales of Peter Parley about America* (Philadelphia: Thomas, Cowperthwait, and Co.: 1847), v.

23 Ibid., 7.

24 Murnaghan and Roberts, *Childhood and the Classics*, p. 134.

25 Sullivan, *Joyce Among the Jesuits*, 45.

26 As Spoo notes, Richmal Mangnall's book, which Joyce had in his Trieste library, is similarly structured, which reinforces the importance of this structure for Stephen. *Joyce and the Language of History*, 44.

27 Spoo, *James Joyce and the Language of History*, 43.

28 Guglielmo Ferrero, *The Greatness and Decline of Rome*, vol. 1, trans. A.E. Zimmern (New York: G.P Putnam's Sons, 1907), iv. Susan Humphreys argues that Joyce incorporated elements of Ferrero's *Il Militarismo* (1898) into Bloom's character. "Ferrero Etc: Joyce's Debt to Guglielmo Ferrero," *James Joyce Quarterly* 16.3 (Spring 1979): 239–51.

29 As Spoo observes, Joyce's exposition of Ferrero's ideas follows directly after his first ever mention of the project that would eventually become *Ulysses* in a letter to Stanislaus dated November 13, 1906 (SL 127–8). See Spoo, *James Joyce and the Language of History*, 31.

30 Ferrero, *The Greatness and Decline of Rome*, vol. 1, vii.

31 Senn, "History as Text in Reverse," 771.

32 See Scholes and Kain, eds. *Workshop of Dedalus*, 99 for Joyce's Trieste notebook, which provides the early material for this passage under the heading "Father William Henry."

33 Gregory Dobbins, *Lazy Idle Schemers: Irish Modernism and the Cultural Politics of Idleness* (Dublin: Field Day Publications, 2010), 5.

34 Ibid., 87.

35 Ibid., 26.

36 Spoo, *James Joyce and the Language of History*, 21.

37 Gifford concludes that this word signals gore not "in the sense of thickened blood or to pierce by a spear or horn but in the obsolete sense of dirt, filth, stain," but the context makes it possible to retain all of the various uses of this word (*UA* 30).

38 Luke Gibbons, "'Old Haunts': Joyce, the Republic, and Photographic Memory," in *Memory Ireland: James Joyce and Cultural Memory*, vol. 4, Oona Frawley, Katherine O'Callaghan, eds. (Syracuse: Syracuse University Press, 2014), 198.

39 Robert Kee, *The Green Flag: A History of Irish Nationalism* (New York: Penguin Books, 2001), 168–9. Qtd. in Vincent Cheng, *Amnesia and the Nation: History, Forgetting, and James Joyce*, (New York: Palgrave Macmillan, 2018), 97.

40 Margaret McBride, "The Ineluctable Modality: Stephen's Request for Immortality," in *James Joyce*, Harold Bloom, ed. (New York: Bloom's Literary Criticism, 2009), 135.

41 Cheng, *Amnesia and the Nation*, 344.

42 Dobbins, *Lazy Idle Schemers*, 97. Dobbins also argues that the dragon womb comes from Milton's "Comus."

43 See Pietro Pucci, *Odysseus Polutropos: Intertextual Readings in the* Odyssey *and the* Iliad (Ithaca: Cornell University Press, 1987), 213 and *The Song of the Sirens: Essays on Homer* (Lanham: Rowman and Littlefield, 1998), 1–9.

44 Andrew Ford, *Homer: The Poetry of the Past* (Ithaca: Cornell University Press, 1992), 85. On the Sirens in relation to the Iliadic Muses, also see Charles Segal, "*Kleos* and Its Ironies in the *Odyssey*." *Classical Antiquity* 52.1 (1983): 40; and Lillian Doherty, *Siren Songs: Gender, Audiences, and Narrators in the* Odyssey (Ann Arbor: University of Michigan Press, 1995).

45 I have written about modernist receptions of the Sirens in "Lost and Found in Translation: The Genesis of Modernism's Siren Songs," in *The Classics in Modernist Translation*, eds. Miranda Hickman and Lynn Kozak (London: Bloomsbury Press, 2019).

46 Gregory Castle, *Reading the Modernist Bildungsroman* (Gainesville: University Press of Florida, 2006), 165.

47 Stephen Kern, *The Culture of Time and Space, 1880–1918* (Cambridge: Harvard University Press, 2003), 55.

3. Joyce, Homer, and the Seductions of Reading

1 Fritz Senn, "One Thinks of Homer," in *Joycean Murmoirs*, ed. Christine O'Neill (Dublin: Lilliput Press, 2007), 75.

2 John Nash, *James Joyce and the Act of Reception*, 62.

3 Although the lectures have themselves not survived, Joyce's notes have. See William Quillian, "Shakespeare in Trieste: Joyce's 1912 *Hamlet* Lectures," *James Joyce Quarterly* 12.1–2 (Fall 1974-Winter 1975): 7–63.

4   Luca Crispi, "Manuscript Timeline, 1905–1922," *Genetic Joyce Studies*, Issue 4 (Spring 2004). www.geneticjoycestudies.org/GJS4/GJS4%20Crispi.htm. See also Michael Groden, Ulysses *in Progress* (Princeton: Princeton University Press, 1977), 17.

5   Although an exhaustive list is not possible, here is a representative sample of important contributions to this discussion in the past century, covering a range of methodologies:

> Stuart Gilbert, *James Joyce's* Ulysses (New York: Random House, 1955); W.B. Stanford, *The* Ulysses *Theme: A Study in the Adaptability of a Traditional Hero* (Oxford: Basil Blackwell, 1954).
>
> Hugh Kenner, "Homer's Sticks and Stones," *James Joyce Quarterly* 6, no. 4 (Summer 1966): 285–98. Kenner, "Uses of Homer," in Kenner, *Ulysses* (Baltimore: Johns Hopkins University Press, 1987), 19–30; Richard Ellmann, "Joyce and Homer," *Critical Inquiry* 3.3 (Spring 1977): 567–82.
>
> R.J. Schork, *Greek and Hellenic Culture in Joyce* (Gainesville: University of Florida Press, 1998);
>
> Michael Seidel, *Epic Geography: James Joyce's* Ulysses (Princeton: Princeton University Press, 1976); Keri Ames, "Joyce's Aesthetic of the Double Negative and His Encounters with Homer's *Odyssey*," in *Beckett, Joyce, and the Art of the Negative*, ed. Colleen Jaurretche (Amsterdam: Rodopi, 2016), 15–48. The ongoing work of Fritz Senn has been important to this conversation for decades. A useful starting point is "Remodelling Homer," in *Inductive Scrutinies: Focus on Joyce*, ed. Christine O'Neill (Dublin: The Lilliput Press, 1995), 111–32. Also see the catalogue of his work by Michael Groden and Wm. Paul Meahan in "Senn-sus: A Passage Index to Fritz Senn's Writing on *Ulysses*," *James Joyce Quarterly* 2/3, no. 1–4 (Fall 2004-Summer 2006): 133–96. David Weir gives a very useful, general overview that would be of great interest to new and experienced readers of Joyce in that it maintains the complexity of Joyce's engagement with Homer in "Homeric Narrative," in Ulysses *Explained: How Homer, Dante, and Shakespeare Inform Joyce's Modernist Vision* (New York: Palgrave Macmillan, 2015), 15–72. A more extensive listing of studies can be found in Bernard McKenna, *James Joyce's* Ulysses: *A Reference Guide* (Westport: Greenwood Press, 2002), 174, n. 2.

6   Kenner, "Homer's Sticks and Stones." Flack, *Modernism and Homer*, chapter 3.

7   Stanford, *The* Ulysses *Theme*, 296, n. 6.

8   See, for example, Pietro Pucci, *The Song of the Sirens: Essays on Homer* (Lanham: Rowman and Littlefield Publishers, 1998); Ruth Scodel, *Listening to Homer: Tradition, Narrative, and Audience* (Ann Arbor: University of Michigan Press, 1998).

9   Michael Seidel, *Epic Geography: James Joyce's* Ulysses (Princeton: Princeton University Press, 1976).

10 Kenner, "Homer's Sticks and Stones."

11 Seidel, *Epic Geography*, 172. Phillip Herring, *Joyce's Notes and Early Drafts for* Ulysses: *Selections from the Buffalo Collection* (Charlottesville: University Press of Virginia, 1977), 18.

12 *Buffalo Notebooks*, p. 23. Joyce is citing Victor Bérard, *Les Phéniciens et l'Odysée* I (Paris: Armand Colin, 1903), 489–90.

13 To avoid unnecessary confusion, I am using the spelling "Alcinous" for the King of Phaecia even though Joyce's gloss copies Bérard's "Alkinoos." "Alcinous" appears in the translations by Charles Lamb, Samuel Butcher and Andrew Lang, Samuel Butler, and William Cowper, all of which Joyce read. It also appears in the translation by Emily Wilson I use in this chapter.

14 Bérard, *Les Phéniciens* vol. 1, 489.

15 Homer, *The Odyssey*. Translated by Samuel Butcher and Andrew Lang (New York: Collier Books, 1909), 113. When I am writing about Joyce reading Homer, I will use this translation because Joyce used it. Later, I will turn to the most recent English translation of the *Odyssey* (by Emily Wilson) to evaluate how *Ulysses* might bring out the *Odyssey*'s attention to reception.

16 Homer, *Odyssey*, trans. Butcher and Lang, 91. Joyce also displayed interest in the Phaeacian ships in a gloss about a passage where Bérard draws connections between Egyptian and Greek history and uses the Phaeacian ships as an example; in notebook VI.D.7, Joyce wrote: "Ulys. Phae galley (52 oars)." Danis Rose and John O'Hanlon, eds. *James Joyce: The Lost Notebook* (Edinburgh: Split Pea Press, 1989), 31. This gloss points to Bérard, *Les Phéniciens*, vol. II, 595.

17 In another context, I have read Joyce's parody of the Butcher and Lang *Odyssey* style in the "Inisfail the Fair" sequence in "Cyclops" as more specifically a parody of their translation of descriptions of Scheria. If my speculation has merit, then the *Odyssey*'s mapping of civilization and savagery onto one another anticipates Joyce's deployment of hypercivilized language to describe the streets of Dublin.

18 Steve Reece elaborates the various violations made by the Phaeacians. See *The Stranger's Welcome: Oral Theory and the Aesthetics of the Homeric Hospitality Scene* (Ann Arbor: The University of Michigan Press, 1993), 104–7. Also see Gilbert Rose, "The Unfriendly Phaeacians," *Transactions and Proceedings of the American Philological Association*, vol. 100 (1969): 387–406.

19 Robert Rabel, "The Art of Creative Listening," in *Approaches to Homer, Ancient and Modern,* ed. Rabel (Barnsley: Classical Press of Wales, 2005), 173.

20 Bruce Louden, *The Odyssey: Structure, Narration, and Meaning* (Baltimore: Johns Hopkins University Press, 2002), 58.

21 Ibid., 61.

22 Unless marked otherwise, translations of the *Odyssey* are from Homer, *The Odyssey*, trans. Emily Wilson (New York: Norton, 2018).

23 This song has generated substantial critical attention. One important conversation centers on whether we are to assume this song actually existed in the Homeric tradition (and would have been familiar to audiences), or whether it is the invention of the poet. See Gregory Nagy, *The Best of the Achaeans: Concepts of the Hero in Archaic Greek Poetry* (Baltimore: Johns Hopkins University Press, 1999), 13–65 for an example of the first position, and Jenny Strauss Clay as an example of the second: *The Wrath of Athena: Gods and Men in the* Odyssey (Lanham: Rowman and Littlefield, 1997), 241–3.

24 Joyce annotated Bérard on this passage, noting "Demodocus sings / dispute of Ul. & Achilles (Od 8)." Danis Rose and John O'Hanlon, eds. *James Joyce: The Lost Notebook, New Evidence on the Genesis of* Ulysses. Edinburgh: Split Pea Press, 1989), 32.

25 Yoav Rinon, "Mise en abyme" and Tragic Signification in the *Odyssey*: The Three Songs of Demodocus." *Mnemosyne* 59, Fasc. 2 (2006): 213–4.

26 Ibid., 210.

27 Irene J.F. de Jong, *A Narratological Commentary on the* Odyssey (Cambridge, Cambridge University Press, 2001), 198.

28 In Menelaus's account, Odysseus is inside of the horse and prevents the other men from crying out when Helen mimics the voices of their wives to expose the trick. Whereas this account is focalized from inside of the horse—which enhances the story's sense of Helen's treachery—Demodocus' account, as Irene de Jong notes, is focalized from a perspective outside of the horse. Irene de Jong, *A Narratological Commentary on the* Odyssey, 216.

29 Likewise, Homeric critics have long been attentive to Odysseus's similarities to epic singers as part of the *Odyssey*'s self-consciousness. See, for example, Bruce Louden, *The Odyssey: Structure, Narration, Meaning*, chapter 3. Simon Goldhill, *The Poet's Voice: Essays on Poetics and Greek Literature* (Cambridge: Cambridge University Press, 1990), chapter 1; Lillian Doherty, *Gender, Audiences, and Narrators in the* Odyssey (Ann Arbor: University of Michigan Press, 1996).

30 Goldhill, *The Poet's Voice*, 56.

31 Glen Most, "The Structure and Function of Odysseus' *Apologoi*," *Transactions of the American Philological Association* 119 (1989), 30.

32 For this passage, I am using Richmond Lattimore's translation because he preserves the caesura of the Greek passage, which helps to underscore the abrupt quality of the transition. Robert Fagles and Robert Fitzgerald also preserve the caesura; Emily Wilson does not. Homer, *The Odyssey*, translated by Richmond Lattimore (New York: HarperCollins, 1967).

33 On this caesura as an exception to the prosodic patterns of the *Odyssey*, see John Peradotto, *Man in the Middle Voice: Name and Narration in the* Odyssey (Princeton: Princeton University Press, 1990), 81.

34 William Shakespeare, *Hamlet* (New Haven: Yale University Press, 2003).

35 For a fascinating intertextual reading of this aspect of *Hamlet* and the *Odyssey*, see Bruce Louden, "Telemachos, the *Odyssey* and *Hamlet*," *Text & Presentation* 11 (2014): 33–50.

36 Norris, *Virgin and Veteran Readings of* Ulysses (New York: Palgrave, 2011), 2.

37 See Richard Ellmann, "The Backgrounds of *Ulysses*," *The Kenyon Review*, Vol. XVI, no. 3 (Summer 1954): 337–86.

38 Helene Foley, "'Reverse Similes' and Sex Roles in the *Odyssey*," *Arethusa* 11 (1978), 8.

39 See, for example, Frederick Ahl and Hanna Roisman, "Friction in Phaeacia," *Odyssey Re-Formed* (Ithaca: Cornell University Press, 1996), 71–91.

40 As Alfred Heubeck and Arie Hoekstra observe, *pathos* was viewed by ancient critics as a unique feature of Homeric epics. Extended similes such as this one intensify and extend the emotion of the scene for the audience. Heubeck and Hoekstra, eds. *A Commentary on Homer's* Odyssey, vol. 1 (Oxford: Oxford University Press, 1990), 381.

41 For background on this statue, see Christine Mitchell Havelock, *The Aphrodite of Knidos and Her Successors: A Historical Review of the Female Nude in Greek Art* (Ann Arbor: University of Michigan Press, 1995).

42 Valérie Bénéjam, "Stephen and the Venus of Praxiteles: The Backside of Aesthetics," in *Cultural Studies of James Joyce*, edited by R.B. Kershner (Amsterdam: Brill, 2016), 68.

43 This release followed a few years after Caroline Alexander published her translation of the *Iliad*, the first translation of that epic done in English by a woman.

44 Wilson, Emily. Twitter Post. March 8, 2018. https://twitter.com/emilyrcwilson/

45 "An Interview with Emily Wilson, Translator of Homer's *Odyssey*," Runciman Award Website. May 24, 2018. http://runcimanaward.org/2018/05/24/an-interview-with-emily-wilson-translator-of-homers-odyssey-part-2/

46 Ibid.

47 See Doherty, *Siren Songs*.

48 Rose and O'Hanlon, *The Lost Notebook*, 38.

49 An important ancient example was Stesichorus's *Pallinode*—a text that was of vital importance to the American poet H.D. in *Helen in Egypt*. Stesichorus (630–550 BC) was said to have written a work that was critical of Helen, which led to him losing his sight. His sight was only restored to him when he reversed his position on her.

His *Pallinode* argued that the real Helen was in Egypt during the war and that a phantom had been in Troy, thus suggesting that men had fought the Trojan War for an illusion. I have written on this subject in *Modernism and Homer*, Chapter 5.

50 Mihoko Suzuki, *Metamorphoses of Helen: Authority, Difference, and the Epic* (Ithaca: Cornell University Press, 2018), p. 2.

51 Michael Groden notes that Joyce's research on Antisthenes doubtless would have drawn his attention to the curiosity that Antisthenes is one of the only people to comment on the word "polytropos." He shows that Antisthenes argues that *polytropos* is not an ethical quality but rather a rhetorical skill denoting Odysseus's ability to adapt his speech to his listeners. He reads this as an important backdrop for "Aeolus" and also notes that this sense of Antisthenes is compatible with Bérard on Aeolus. Groden, Ulysses *in Progress* (Princeton: Princeton University Press, 1977), 92. Also, see W.B. Stanford, *The* Ulysses *Theme*, 99.

52 The trail of spoken and written comments Joyce left on the *Odyssey* suggests his interest in the trick of the wooden horse. For example, Georges Borach noted in a journal entry dated August 1, 1917 that Joyce identified the theme of the *Odyssey* as "the most human in world literature." He elaborated this thought in the following way: "Before Troy the heroes shed their lifeblood in vain. They want to raise the siege. Ulysses opposes the idea. [He thinks up] the stratagem of the wooden horse. After Troy there is no further talk of Achilles, Menelaus, Agamemnon. Only one man is not done with; his heroic career has hardly begun: Ulysses" (*JJ* 416–7). Joyce here identifies the stratagem—a word he takes from both Samuel Butler and Charles Lamb's translations of descriptions of this scene—as a way of asserting intellect against violence in order to redefine the terms of the heroic for a war-torn culture, a project that resonates with his own work in relation to a period of national and global uprising and war.

53 Schork, *Greek and Hellenic Culture in Joyce*, 85. Immediately following this, he writes an alternate version—"*doureion hippon*" (made of lumber). Odysseus uses this phrase—*Odyssey* 8.492–3 and 8.512—at the court of Alcinous when he asks Demodocus to sing of the Trojan Horse. Schork, *Greek and Hellenic Culture in Joyce*, 86.

54 Kenner, *Dublin's Joyce* (New York: Columbia University Press, 1956), 117. I thank Vicki Mahaffey for bringing this connection to my attention.

55 One major source of instability in his reading of Odysseus concerns the slaughter of the suitors, which seemed to Joyce uncharacteristic of Odysseus. I have written about this in Chapter 3 of *Modernism and Homer*.

56 National Library of Ireland, The Joyce Papers 2002, Notebook II.i.1.

57 Phillip Herring, ed. *James Joyce's Notes and Early Drafts for* Ulysses: *Selections from the Buffalo Collection* (Charlottesville: University of Virginia Press, 1977), 17.

58 I thank Stephanie Nelson for pointing this connection out to me at the International Joyce Symposium, June 16, 2018.

59 Hugh Kenner's work disagrees with my assertion about the underlying importance of Butler's work to *Ulysses*: "The author of the *Odyssey*, he claimed, was a woman and herself the model of the Princess Nausicaa. He could have been a Bentley or a Wolf, inventor of the Homer of his age. Instead he chose to be a man with a silly bee in his bonnet about a poetess, and that his most serious reader should have been James Joyce was perhaps more than he deserved to expect. Joyce with his usual thoroughness acknowledged the mad idea by putting his Nausicaa into the idiom of a lady novelist, and tied bows in it when he allowed readers of *Ulysses* to conclude that its author in turn had modelled on himself a different secondary character, Telemachus, and then had his Telemachus explain, at 2 p.m. in the National Library, Dublin, that the author of *Hamlet* was not to be discovered in the Prince but in the Ghost." *The Pound Era* (Berkeley: University of California Press, 1973), 49.

60 Seidel, *Epic Geography*, 84.

61 Butler, *The Authoress of the* Odyssey (London, 1897), 126.

62 Ibid., 128.

Epilogue: The Pleasures of (Not) Reading Joyce and the Classics

1 Eimear McBride, "My Hero: James Joyce," *The Guardian* (June 6, 2014). Accessed online on March 14, 2019. www.theguardian.com/books/2014/jun/06/my-hero-eimear-mcbride-james-joyce.

2 Ibid.

3 Derek Walcott, *Omeros* (New York: Farrar, Straus, and Giroux, 1992), 200.

4 Derek Walcott, "Another Life Manuscript," MS One 93 (Mona, Jamaica: University of West Indies). Qtd. in Maria McGarrity, "Imagining the 'wettest indies': The Transatlantic Network of James Joyce and Derek Walcott," in Martha C. Carpentier, ed. *Joycean Legacies* (London: Palgrave Macmillan, 2015), 214.

5 Qtd. in McGarrity, "Transatlantic Network," 213.

6 Dennis O'Driscoll, *Stepping Stones: Interviews with Seamus Heaney* (New York: Farrar, Straus and Giroux, 2008), 249–50.

7 Eileen Battersby, "A Greek Tragedy for Our Times," *Irish Times* (April 3, 2004). www.irishtimes.com/news/a-greek-tragedy-for-our-times-1.1138235.

8 Colum McCann, "But Always Meeting Ourselves." *New York Times* (June 15, 2009). www.nytimes.com/2009/06/16/opinion/16mccann.html.

9   Gabriel García Márquez, *Living to Tell the Tale, vol. 1,* trans. Edith Grossman (New York: Vintage International, 2004), 271.

10 Beth Blum, "*Ulysses* as Self-Help Manual?: James Joyce's Strategic Populism," *Modern Language Quarterly* 74, no. 1 (2013), 69.

11 See www.mayalang.com/book/ulysses-references/

12 Sean Latham, *Am I a Snob*, 168.

13 Ariela Freedman, "Drawing on Modernism in Alison Bechdel's 'Fun Home'," *Journal of Modern Literature* 32, no. 4 (Summer 2009), 130.

14 Hilary Chute, "Gothic Revival," *Village Voice* (July 4, 2006). www.villagevoice.com/2006/07/04/gothic-revival-2. Also qtd in Freedman, "Drawing on Modernism," 127.

15 Bechdel has commented widely on this aspect of her process. This particular statement comes from Oliver Burkeman, "A Life Stripped Bare," *The Guardian* October 16, 2006. www.theguardian.com/books/2006/oct/16/biography.oliverburkeman

16 Scott McCloud, *Understanding Comics: The Invisible Art* (New York: HarperCollins, 1994), 36.

17 Bechdel notes in an interview with Hilary Chute that she draws in the "usual cartoony style" 1009. Qtd. in Jennifer Lemberg, "Closing the Gap in Alison Bechdel's 'Fun Home'," *Women's Studies Quarterly* 1/2 (Spring-Summer 2008), 129.

18 McCloud, *Understanding Comics*, 36.

19 Ibid, 69.

20 Forrest Read, ed. *Pound/Joyce Letters* (New York: New Directions, 1967), 250.

21 For an argument against this position, see John Nash, *James Joyce and the Act of Reception*, 6.

Bibliography

Ahl, Frederick and Hanna Roisman. "Friction in Phaeacia" in *Odyssey Re-Formed*. Ithaca: Cornell University Press, 1996, 71–91.

Aldington, Richard. "Anti-Hellenism: A Note on Some Modern Art," *The Egoist* 2, no. 1 (January 15, 1914), 36.

Aldington, Richard. "Le Latin Mystique," *The Egoist*, March 16, 1914.

Aldington, Richard. "The Influence of Mr. James Joyce," *English Review* 32 (April 1921), 333–41.

Ames, Keri. "Joyce's Aesthetic of the Double Negative and His Encounters with Homer's *Odyssey*." In *Beckett, Joyce, and the Art of the Negative*. Edited by Colleen Jaurretche (Amsterdam: Rodopi, 2016), 15–48.

Angeli, Diego. "An Italian Comment on *Portrait*." Translated by James Joyce. *The Egoist* 5, no. 2 (February 1918), 30.

"Aramis." "The Scandal of *Ulysses*," *Sporting Times*, no. 34 (April 1, 1922), 4.

Auerbach, Erich. *Mimesis: The Representation of Reality in Western Literature*. Princeton: Princeton University Press, 1968.

Backus, Margot and Joseph Valente. "'An Encounter': James Joyce's Humiliation Nation." In *Collaborative Dubliners: Joyce in Dialogue*. Edited by Vicki Mahaffey. Syracuse: Syracuse University Press, 2012.

Bakhtin, M.M. *The Dialogic Imagination*. Edited by Michael Holquist. Translated by Caryl Emerson and Michael Holquist. Austin: University of Texas Press, 1982.

Baldick, Chris. *The Oxford Dictionary of Literary Terms*, 3rd edition. 2008. Online version accessed May 10, 2018.

Battersby, Eileen. "A Greek Tragedy for Our Times," *Irish Times*. April 3, 2004. www.irishtimes.com/news/a-greek-tragedy-for-our-times-1.1138235.

Bénéjam, Valérie. "Stephen and the Venus of Praxiteles: The Backside of Aesthetics." In *Cultural Studies of James Joyce*. Edited by R.B. Kershner. Amsterdam: Brill, 2016, 59–76.

Benstock, Bernard. "Inscribing James Joyce's Tombstone." In *Coping with Joyce: Essays from the Copenhagen Symposium*. Edited by Morris Beja and Shari Benstock. Columbus: The Ohio State University Press, 1989, 73–90.

Bérard, Victor. *Les Phéniciens et l'Odysée* I. Paris: Armand Colin, 1903.

Bersani, Leo. "Against Ulysses." In *James Joyce's* Ulysses: *A Casebook*. Edited by Derek Attridge. Oxford: Oxford University Press, 2004, 201–30.

Blum, Beth. "*Ulysses* as Self-Help Manual? James Joyce's Strategic Populism." *Modern Language Quarterly* 74, vol. 1 (2013), 67–93.

Boswell, James. *The Life of Samuel Johnson, vol. 2.* New York: Harper, 1859.

Bradley, Bruce, S.J. *James Joyce's Schooldays.* New York: St. Martin's Press, 1982.

Bradley, Bruce, S.J. "At School Together in Conmee's Time: Some Notes on Joyce's Clongowes Jesuit." *Dublin James Joyce Journal* 3 (2010), 1–18.

Brown, Richard. *James Joyce and Sexuality.* Cambridge: Cambridge University Press, 1985.

Budgen, Frank. *James Joyce and the Making of* Ulysses. Oxford: Oxford University Press, 1972.

Burkeman, Oliver. "A Life Stripped Bare," *The Guardian* October 16, 2006. www.theguardian.com/books/2006/oct/16/biography.oliverburkeman

Butler, Christopher. "Joyce, the Modernist." *Cambridge Companion to James Joyce.* Edited by Derek Attridge. Cambridge: Cambridge University Press, 2004, 67–86.

Butler, Samuel. *The Authoress of the* Odyssey. London, 1897.

Byrne, J.F. *Silent Years: An Autobiography with Memoirs of James Joyce and Our Ireland.* New York: Farrar, Straus & Young, 1953.

Carpentier, Martha, Ed. *Joycean Legacies.* London: Palgrave Macmillan, 2015.

Castle, Gregory. *Reading the Modernist Bildungsroman.* Gainesville: University Press of Florida, 2006.

Cheng, Vincent. *Joyce, Race, and Empire.* Cambridge: Cambridge University Press, 1995.

Cheng, Vincent. *Amnesia and the Nation: History, Forgetting, and James Joyce.* New York: Palgrave Macmillan, 2018.

Chute, Hilary. "Gothic Revival," *Village Voice.* July 4, 2006. www.villagevoice.com/2006/07/04/gothic-revival-2

Clay, Jenny Strauss. *The Wrath of Athena: Gods and Men in the* Odyssey. Lanham: Rowman and Littlefield, 1997.

Corcoran, William, S.J., *Studies in the History of Classical Teaching.* New York: Benzinger Brothers, 1911.

Cox, Fiona. *Ovid's Presence in Contemporary Women's Writing: Strange Monsters.* Oxford: Oxford University Press, 2018.

Crispi, Luca. "Manuscript Timeline, 1905–1922," *Genetic Joyce Studies*, Issue 4 (Spring 2004). www.geneticjoycestudies.org/GJS4/GJS4%20Crispi.htm

Culleton, Claire and Ellen Scheible. *Rethinking Joyce's* Dubliners. New York: Palgrave, 2017.

de Jong, Irene J.F. *A Narratological Commentary on the* Odyssey. Cambridge, Cambridge University Press, 2001.

Deming, Robert H. *James Joyce: The Critical Heritage.* London: Routledge, 1997.

Dettmar, Kevin. "'Working in Accord with Obstacles': A Postmodern Perspective on Joyce's 'Mythical Method.'" In *Re-reading the New: A Backward Glance at Modernism*. Edited by Dettmar. Ann Arbor: University of Michigan Press, 1992, 277–96.

Dettmar, Kevin. *The Illicit Joyce of Postmodernism: Reading Against the Grain*. Madison: University of Wisconsin Press, 1996.

Diepeeven, Leonard. *The Difficulties of Modernism*. New York: Routledge, 2003.

Dillon, Joe. "The Classics at the Wake: Some Aspects of Classical Influence in Joyce's *Finnegans Wake*." *Classics Ireland*, vol. 5 (1998): 9–29.

Dimock, George. "The Name of Odysseus" *Hudson Review* 9, no. 1 (Spring 1956): 54–57.

Dobbins, Gregory. *Lazy Idle Schemers: Irish Modernism and the Cultural Politics of Idleness*. Dublin: Field Day Publications, 2010.

Doherty, Lillian. *Siren Songs: Gender, Audiences, and Narrators in the* Odyssey. Ann Arbor: University of Michigan Press, 1996.

Doyle, Charles. *Richard Aldington: A Biography*. Carbondale: Southern Illinois University, 1989.

Eliot, T.S. "*Ulysses*, Order, and Myth," *Selected Prose of T.S. Eliot*. Edited by Frank Kermode. London: Faber, 1975, 175–7.

Ellmann, Richard. "The Backgrounds of *Ulysses*," *The Kenyon Review*, vol. XVI, no. 3 (Summer 1954): 337–86.

Ellmann, Richard. "Joyce and Homer," *Critical Inquiry* 3.3 (Spring 1977): 567–82.

Fargnoli, A. Nicholas and Michael Patrick Gillespie, *A Critical Companion to James Joyce*. New York: Facts on File, 2006.

Farrell, Joseph. "Joyce and Modernist Latinity." In William Brickliss, et al., Eds. *Reception and the Classics*. Cambridge: Cambridge University Press, 2012, 57–72.

Ferrero, Guglielmo. *The Greatness and Decline of Rome*, vol. 1. Trans. A.E. Zimmern. New York: G.P Putnam's Sons, 1907.

Flack, Leah Culligan. "'Cyclops,' Censorship, and Joyce's Monster Audiences." *James Joyce Quarterly* 48, no. 3 (Spring 2011), 425–444.

Flack, Leah Culligan, *Modernism and Homer: The Odysseys of H.D., James Joyce, Osip Mandelstam, and Ezra Pound*. Cambridge: Cambridge University Press, 2015.

Flack, Leah Culligan. "Lost and Found in Translation: The Genesis of Modernism's Siren Songs." In *The Classics in Modernist Translation*. Edited by Miranda Hickman and Lynn Kozak. London: Bloomsbury Academic, 2019.

Foley, Helene. "'Reverse Similes' and Sex Roles in the *Odyssey*." *Arethusa* 11 (1978): 7–26.

Ford, Andrew. *Homer: The Poetry of the Past*. Ithaca: Cornell University Press, 1992.

Freedman, Ariela. "Drawing on Modernism in Alison Bechdel's 'Fun Home'." *Journal of Modern Literature* 32, no. 4 (Summer 2009): 125–40.

Gibbons, Luke. "'Old Haunts': Joyce, the Republic, and Photographic Memory." In *Memory Ireland: James Joyce and Cultural Memory*, vol. 4. Edited by Oona Frawley and Katherine O'Callaghan. Syracuse: Syracuse University Press, 2014.

Gibson, Andrew. *Joyce's Revenge: History, Politics, and Aesthetics in* Ulysses. Oxford: Oxford University Press, 2002.

Gilbert, Stuart. *James Joyce's* Ulysses. New York, Vintage, 1955.

Gilbert, Stuart and Wm. Paul Meahan, "Senn-sus: A Passage Index to Fritz Senn's Writing on *Ulysses*," *James Joyce Quarterly* 2/3, no. 1–4 (Fall 2004–Summer 2006): 133–96.

Gillespie, Michael Patrick. *James Joyce and the Exilic Imagination*. Gainesville: University of Florida Press, 2015.

Goldhill, Simon. *The Poet's Voice: Essays on Poetics and Greek Literature*. Cambridge: Cambridge University Press, 1990.

Goodrich, Samuel Griswold. *Peter Parley's Tales of Greece and Rome*. London: Gresham Publishing.

Goodrich, Samuel Griswold. *Tales of Peter Parley about America*. Philadelphia: Thomas, Cowperthwait, and Co. 1847.

Groden, Michael. Ulysses *in Progress*. Princeton: Princeton University Press, 1977.

Hall, Edith and Justine McConnell, Eds. *Ancient Greek Myth in World Fiction since 1989*. London: Bloomsbury Academic, 2016.

Hardwick, Lorna and Christopher Stray, *Reception Studies*. Oxford: Oxford University Press, 2003.

Hardwick, Lorna and Christopher Stray, *A Companion to Classical Receptions*. Oxford: Blackwell, 2008.

Havelock, Christine Mitchell. *The Aphrodite of Knidos and Her Successors: A Historical Review of the Female Nude in Greek Art*. Ann Arbor: University of Michigan Press, 2007.

Haynes, Kenneth. "Gentleman's Latin, Lady's Greek," *The Oxford Companion to the Victorian Novel*. Edited by Lisa Rodensky, Oxford University Press, 2013, 413–37.

Hayot, Eric. "The Sky Is Falling." *Profession*, Humanities Commons, Modern Languages Association (May 21, 2018). Web. Accessed October 15, 2018.

Heaney, Seamus. *Station Island*. London: Faber and Faber, 1985.

Heaney, Seamus. "Crediting Poetry." In *Opened Ground: Selected Poems, 1966–1996*. New York: Farrar, Straus, and Giroux, 1996, 445–67.

Herring, Phillip, Ed. *James Joyce's Notes and Early Drafts for* Ulysses: *Selections from the Buffalo Collection*. Charlottesville: University of Virginia Press, 1977.

Heubeck, Alfred and Arie Hoekstra, Eds. *A Commentary on Homer's* Odyssey, vol. 1. Oxford: Oxford University Press, 1990.

Hickman, Miranda and Lynn Kozak, Eds. *The Classics in Modernist Translation*. London: Bloomsbury, 2019.

Homer. *The Odyssey*. Translated by Samuel Butcher and Andrew Lang. New York: Collier Books, 1909.

Homer. *The Odyssey*. Translated by Richmond Lattimore. New York: HarperCollins, 1967.

Homer. *The Odyssey*. Translated by Emily Wilson. New York: Norton, 2018.

Howard, Jennifer. "Status of the Humanities: We Haven't Quite Recovered from the Recession," *The Chronicle of Higher Education* (June 19, 2014). Web. Accessed October 9, 2018.

Hulme, T.E. *Speculations: Essays on Humanism and the Philosophy of Art*. Edited by Hubert Read. London: Routledge, 1960.

Humphreys, Susan. "Ferrero Etc: Joyce's Debt to Guglielmo Ferrero." *James Joyce Quarterly* 16.3 (Spring 1979): 239–51.

Hutton, Clare. "Joyce and the Institutions of Revivalism." *Irish University Review* 33, no. 1 (Spring–Summer 2003): 117–32.

Ingleheart, Jennifer. *Masculine Plural: Queer Classics, Sex, and Education*. Oxford: Oxford University Press, 2018.

Jacobus, Lee A. "'Lycidas' in the 'Nestor' Episode." *James Joyce Quarterly*, vol. 19, no. 2 (Winter, 1982): 189–94.

James, David, Ed. *The Legacies of Modernism: Historicising Postwar and Contemporary Fiction*. Cambridge: Cambridge University Press, 2011.

James, David. *Modernist Futures: Innovation and Inheritance in the Contemporary Novel*. Cambridge: Cambridge University Press, 2012.

Joyce, James. *A Portrait of the Artist as a Young Man*. Edited by Jean Paul Riquelme. New York: Norton, 2007.

Joyce, James. *Dubliners*. New York: Norton, 2006.

Joyce, James. James Joyce Papers, Harry Ransom Center, University of Texas at Austin.

Joyce, James. National Library of Ireland, The Joyce Papers 2002, Notebook II.i.1.

Joyce, James. *Selected Letters*. Edited by Richard Ellmann. New York: Viking Press, 1957.

Joyce, James. *Stephen Hero*. New York: New Directions, 1963.

Joyce, James. *The Critical Writings*. Edited by Ellsworth Mason and Richard Ellmann. New York. Viking Press, 1959.

Joyce, James. *Ulysses*. New York: Vintage Books, 1986.

Joyce, Stanislaus. *My Brother's Keeper: James Joyce's Early Years*. Cambridge, MA: DeCapo Press, 1958.

Kee, Robert. *The Green Flag: A History of Irish Nationalism*. New York: Penguin Books, 2001.

Kenner, Hugh. *Dublin's Joyce*. New York: Columbia University Press, 1956.

Kenner, Hugh. "Homer's Sticks and Stones," *James Joyce Quarterly* 6, no. 4 (Summer 1966): 285–98.

Kenner, Hugh. *The Pound Era*. Berkeley: University of California Press, 1973.

Kenner, Hugh. *Ulysses*. Baltimore: Johns Hopkins University Press, 1987.

Kenner, Hugh. "On the Centenary of James Joyce." *New York Times*. January 31, 1982. www.nytimes.com/books/00/01/09/specials/joyce-centenary.html. Accessed October 28, 2016.

Kershner, R. Brandon. *Joyce, Bakhtin, and Popular Culture: Chronicles of Disorder*. Chapel Hill: University of North Carolina Press, 1989.

Kiberd, Declan. Ulysses *and Us: The Art of Everyday Life in Joyce's Masterpiece*. New York: Norton, 2010.

Latham, Sean. *Am I a Snob? Modernism and the Novel*. Ithaca: Cornell University Press, 2003.

Latham, Sean and Gayle Rogers, *Modernism: The Evolution of an Idea*. Bloomsbury: Bloomsbury Press, 2015.

Lawrence, Karen. *The Odyssey of Style in* Ulysses. Princeton: Princeton University Press, 1981.

Lawton, Phillip. "For the gentleman and the scholar: Sexual and Scatological References in the Loeb Classical Library." In *Expurgating the Classics: Editing Out in Greek or Latin*. Edited by Steven Harrison and Christopher Stray. London: Bloomsbury Academic, 2012, 175–96.

Lemberg, Jennifer. "Closing the Gap in Alison Bechdel's 'Fun Home.'" *Women's Studies Quarterly* 1/2 (Spring–Summer 2008), 129–40.

Levenson, Michael. "Modernisms." In *James Joyce in Context*. Edited by John McCourt. Cambridge: Cambridge University Press, 2009, 262–74.

Louden, Bruce. *The Odyssey: Structure, Narration, and Meaning*. Baltimore: Johns Hopkins University Press, 2002.

Louden, Bruce. "Telemachos, the *Odyssey* and *Hamlet*," *Text & Presentation* 11 (2014): 33–50.

MacCabe, Colin. *On the Eloquence of the Vulgar: Language, Cinema, and the Politics of Culture*. London: Bloomsbury Press, 1999.

Mahaffey, Vicki and Michael Groden. "Silence and Fractals in 'The Sisters.'" In *Collaborative Dubliners: Joyce in Dialogue*, Ed. Mahaffey. Syracuse: Syracuse University Press, 2012.

Mahaffy, John Pentland. *Social Life in Greece: From Homer to Menander*. London: Macmillan, 1877.

Majumdar, Saikat. *Prose of the World: Modernism and the Banality of Empire*. Columbia: Columbia University Press, 2013.

Mamigonian, Marc and Joel Turner. "Annotations to *Stephen Hero*," *James Joyce Quarterly* 40, no. 3 (Spring 2003), 347–518.

Mao, Douglas and Rebecca Walkowitz, "The New Modernist Studies," *PMLA* 123, no. 3 (May 2008), 737–48.

Marshik, Celia. *British Modernism and Censorship*. Cambridge: Cambridge University Press, 2006.

Martz, Louis L. "Who Is Lycidas?" *Yale French Studies*, no. 47, *Image and Symbol in the Renaissance* (1972): 170–88.

Márquez, Gabriel García. *Living to Tell the Tale, vol. 1*. Translated by Edith Grossman. New York: Vintage International, 2004.

McArthur, Murray. "'The Index Nothing Affirmeth': The Semiotic Formation of a Literary Mandate in James Joyce's 'The Sisters,'" *James Joyce Quarterly* 45, no. 2. (Winter 2008), 245–62.

McBride, Eimear. "My Hero: James Joyce," *The Guardian*. June 6, 2014. www.theguardian.com/books/2014/jun/06/my-hero-eimear-mcbride-james-joyce

McBride, Margaret. "The Ineluctable Modality: Stephen's Request for Immortality." In *James Joyce*. Harold Bloom, Ed. New York: Bloom's Literary Criticism, 2009, 117–40.

McCann, Colum. "But Always Meeting Ourselves." *New York Times*. June 15, 2009. www.nytimes.com/2009/06/16/opinion/16mccann.html.

McCloud, Scott. *Understanding Comics: The Invisible Art*. New York: HarperCollins, 1994.

McDonald, Rónán. "The Irish Revival and Modernism," in *The Cambridge Companion to Irish Modernism*. Cambridge: Cambridge University Press, 2014, 51–62.

McGarrity, Maria. "Imagining the 'wettest indies': The Transatlantic Network of James Joyce and Derek Walcott." In *Joycean Legacies*. Edited by Martha Carpentier. New York: Palgrave Macmillan, 2015, 213–29.

Most, Glen. "The Structure and Function of Odysseus' *Apologoi*," *Transactions of the American Philological Association* 119 (1989), 15–30.

Mullin, Katherine. *James Joyce, Sexuality, and Social Purity*. Cambridge: Cambridge University Press, 2003.

Murnaghan, Sheila and Deborah H. Roberts, *Childhood and the Classics, Britain and America 1850–1965*. Oxford: Oxford University Press, 2018.

Murphy, Sean P. *James Joyce and Victims: Reading the Logic of Exclusion*. Fairleigh Dickinson University Press, 2003.

Nagy, Gregory. *The Best of the Achaeans: Concepts of the Hero in Archaic Greek Poetry*. Baltimore: Johns Hopkins University Press, 1999.

Nash, John. *James Joyce and the Act of Reception: Reading, Ireland, Modernism*. Cambridge: Cambridge University Press, 2006.

Nolan, Emer. "Modernism and the Irish Revival." In Joe Cleary and Claire Connolly, Eds. *The Cambridge Companion to Modern Irish Culture*. Cambridge: Cambridge University Press, 2005, 157–72.

Norris, Margot. "A Walk on the Wild(e) Side: the Doubled Reading of 'An Encounter.'" In *Quare Joyce*, edited by Joseph Valente. Ann Arbor: University of Michigan Press, 1998, 19–34.

Norris, Margot. *Suspicious Reading of Joyce's* Dubliners. Philadelphia: University of Pennsylvania Press, 2003.

Norris, Margot. *Virgin and Veteran Readings of* Ulysses. New York: Palgrave, 2011.

O'Driscoll, Dennis. *Stepping Stones: Interviews with Seamus Heaney.* New York: Farrar, Straus and Giroux, 2008.

Peradotto, John. *Man in the Middle Voice: Name and Narration in the* Odyssey. Princeton: Princeton University Press, 1990.

Platt, Len. *Joyce and the Anglo-Irish: A Study of Joyce and the Literary Revival.* Amsterdam: Rodopi, 1998.

Pound, Ezra. *Literary Essays.* Edited by T.S. Eliot. New York, New Directions, 1935.

Pound, Ezra. *Selected Letters 1907–1941.* Edited by D.D. Paige. New York: New Directions, 1950.

Power, Mary. "The Discovery of Ruby." *James Joyce Quarterly* 18.2 (Winter 1981), 115–21.

Powers, Melinda. *Diversifying Greek Tragedy on the American Stage.* Oxford: Oxford University Press, 2018.

Pucci, Pietro. *Odysseus Polutropos: Intertextual Readings in the* Odyssey *and the* Iliad. Ithaca: Cornell University Press, 1987.

Pucci, Pietro. *The Song of the Sirens: Essays on Homer.* Lanham: Rowman and Littlefield Publishers, 1998.

Quillian, William. "Shakespeare in Trieste: Joyce's 1912 *Hamlet* Lectures," *James Joyce Quarterly* 12.1–2 (Fall 1974–Winter 1975): 7–63.

Rabaté, Jean-Michel. "On Joycean and Wildean Sodomy." In *Quare Joyce*, edited by Joseph Valente. Ann Arbor: University of Michigan Press, 1998, 35–46.

Rabel, Robert. "The Art of Creative Listening." In *Approaches to Homer, Ancient and Modern.* Edited by Robert Rabel. Barnsley: Classical Press of Wales, 2005, 167–88.

Read, Forrest, Ed. *Pound/Joyce Letters.* New York: New Directions, 1967.

Ready, W.B. "Review of *Silent Years.*" *America* (May 15, 1954).

Reece, Steve. *The Stranger's Welcome: Oral Theory and the Aesthetics of the Homeric Hospitality Scene.* Ann Arbor: The University of Michigan Press, 1993.

Reynolds, Paige. *Modernist Afterlives in Irish Literature and Culture.* London: Anthem Press, 2016.

Rinon, Yoav. "'Mise en abyme' and Tragic Signification in the *Odyssey*: The Three Songs of Demodocus," *Mnemosyne* 59, Fasc. 2 (2006): 208–25.

Rogers, Brett M. and Benjamin Eldon Stevens, Eds. *Once and Future Antiquities in Science Fiction and Fantasy.* London: Bloomsbury Academic Press, 2018.

Rose, Danis and John O'Hanlon, Eds. *James Joyce: The Lost Notebook, New Evidence on the Genesis of* Ulysses. Edinburgh: Split Pea Press, 1989.

Rose, Gilbert. "The Unfriendly Phaeacians," *Transactions and Proceedings of the American Philological Association*, vol. 100 (1969): 387–406.

Rubenstein, Michael. *Public Works: Infrastructure, Irish Modernism, and the Postcolonial*. South Bend: University of Notre Dame Press, 2010.

Rubenstein, Michael. "City Circuits: 'Aeolus' and 'Wandering Rocks.'" In *The Cambridge Companion to* Ulysses, edited by Sean Latham. Cambridge: Cambridge University Press, 2014, 113–27.

Schein, Seth. "'Our Debt to Greece and Rome': Canon, Class, and Ideology." In Lorna Hardwick and Christopher Stray, Eds., *A Companion to Classical Receptions*. Oxford: Blackwell, 2008.

Scholes, Robert E. and Richard Morgan Kain, Eds. *The Workshop of Dedalus: James Joyce and the Raw Materials for* A Portrait of the Artist as a Young Man. Evanston: Northwestern University Press, 1965.

Schork, R.J. *Greek and Hellenic Culture in Joyce*. Gainesville: University Press of Florida, 1998.

Schork, R.J. *Latin and Roman Culture in Joyce*. Gainesville: University Press of Florida, 1997.

Scodel, Ruth. *Listening to Homer: Tradition, Narrative, and Audience*. Ann Arbor: University of Michigan Press, 1998.

Segal, Charles. "*Kleos* and Its Ironies in the *Odyssey*." *Classical Antiquity* 52.1. (1983): 22–47.

Seidel, Michael. *Epic Geography: James Joyce's* Ulysses. Princeton: Princeton University Press, 1976).

Senn, Fritz. "The Challenge: 'Ignotas Animum' (An Old-Fashioned Close-Guessing at a Borrowed Structure)," *James Joyce Quarterly* 16, no. 1–2 (Fall 1978–Winter 1979): 123–34.

Senn, Fritz. "History as Text in Reverse," *James Joyce Quarterly*, vol. 28, no. 4 (Summer 1991): 765–75.

Senn, Fritz. "Remodelling Homer," in *Inductive Scrutinies: Focus on Joyce*. Edited by Christine O'Neill. Dublin: The Lilliput Press, 1995, 111–32.

Senn, Fritz. "Gnomon Inverted." In *ReJoycing: New Readings of* Dubliners. Edited by Rosa Bollettieri Bosinelli and Harold F. Mosher. Louisville: University of Kentucky Press, 1998, 248–57.

Senn, Fritz. "One Thinks of Homer." In *Joycean Murmoirs*. Edited by Christine O'Neill. Dublin: Lilliput Press, 2007.

Shakespeare, William. *Hamlet*. New Haven: Yale University Press, 2003.

Sheehy, Eugene. *The Joyce We Knew*, Ed. Ulick O'Connor. Cork: Mercier Press, 1967.

Spurr, David. "How to Read *Ulysses*." Review of Declan Kiberd, Ulysses *and Us*, 2009. *James Joyce Broadsheet* 84 (October 2009): 1.

Stanford, W.B. *The* Ulysses *Theme: A Study in the Adaptability of a Traditional Hero*. Oxford: Basil Blackwell, 1954.

Stanford, W.B. *Ireland and the Classical Tradition*. Dublin: Allen Figgis, 1976.

Stray, Christopher. *Classics Transformed: Schools, Universities, and Society in England 1830–1960*. Oxford: Clarendon Press, 1998.

Sullivan, Kevin. *Joyce Among the Jesuits*. New York: Columbia University Press, 1958.

Suzuki, Mihoko. *Metamorphoses of Helen: Authority, Difference, and the Epic*. Ithaca: Cornell University Press, 2018.

Tully, Nola, Ed. *Yes I Said Yes I Will Yes: A Celebration of James Joyce,* Ulysses, *and 100 Years of Bloomsday*. New York, Vintage Books, 2004.

Valente, Joseph. "'Thrilled by his touch': the Aestheticizing of Homosexual Panic in *A Portrait of the Artist as a Young Man*." In *Quare Joyce*, edited by Valente. Ann Arbor: University of Michigan Press, 1998, 47–76.

Vanderham, Paul. *James Joyce and Censorship: The Trials of* Ulysses. London: Palgrave Macmillan UK, 1997.

Walcott, Derek. *Omeros*. New York: Farrar, Straus, and Giroux, 1992.

Waquet, Francoise. *Latin, or The Empire of the Sign: From the Sixteenth to the Twentieth Centuries*. New York and London: Verso Books, 2002.

Weir, David. "Homeric Narrative." In Ulysses *Explained: How Homer, Dante, and Shakespeare Inform Joyce's Modernist Vision*. New York: Palgrave Macmillan, 2015, 15–72.

Wilde, Oscar. *The Women of Homer*. London: The Oscar Wilde Society, 2008.

Williams, Trevor. "Conmeeism and the Universe of Discourse in 'Wandering Rocks,'" *James Joyce Quarterly* 29, no. 2. (Winter, 1992): 267–79.

Wilson, Emily. "An Interview with Emily Wilson, Translator of Homer's *Odyssey*," Runciman Award Website. May 24, 2018. http://runcimanaward.org/2018/05/24/an-interview-with-emily-wilson-translator-of-homers-odyssey-part-2/

Ziolkowski, Theodore. *Classicism of the Twenties*. Chicago: University of Chicago Press 2015.

Index